WISDOM TO A
SUSTAINABLE
JOURNEY

NIRMAL K MANDAL &
NILENDU MUKHERJEE

INDIA · SINGAPORE · MALAYSIA

Notion Press

No. 8, 3rd Cross Street,
CIT Colony, Mylapore,
Chennai, Tamil Nadu – 600 004

First Published by Notion Press 2020
Copyright © Nirmal K Mandal & Nilendu Mukherjee 2020
All Rights Reserved.

ISBN 978-1-64951-619-0

We dedicate this book to...

*Health care service providers around the globe for their relentless
services to save the lives of people across the world during the COVID-19 Pandemic.*

Contents

Acknowledgement

From Nirmal:

To the almighty for choicest blessings

&

To my spiritual Master-Bhagwan ji for wisdom that I treasure and her choicest blessings

To my mother-Ramani for her blessings, love, and support

To my wife Asima and my son, Arnav, for their inspiration and support

To my friend Pat Naicker for her inspiration and good advice

To Margaret Rose Rosario for editorial support

To Samikshya for the cover page design

To Samikshya, Shruti, Arpita and Rajendran for providing support in creative arts

From Nilendu:

To the almighty for choicest blessings

&

To my parents Uma and Nalinaksha Mukherjee for their blessings and love.

To my Grandfather-Late Dr Shanti Ranjan Sur
(Freedom Fighter) for his love and affection.

To my wife, Seoni and my daughter, Shaivi for
their inspiration and support

to my younger brother Advocate Niladri Mukherjee
& his family for being a part in this journey.

To all my friends and colleagues for their care, and all the team
members of this book, for their relentless work.

Preface

The Journey was longer than expected. Nilendu and I had met nearly 15 years back, incidentally, for the first time, to discuss work, and we had it completed with a rigorous experiential learning to understand the value chain of agriculture produces of poor farmers in erstwhile Andhra Pradesh (Now Telangana state). A little further value-add was achieved during our regular work in the development sector. During that period, we met several times. Fortunately, on one such occasion, we became a part of it as contributors along with a few others, for a textbook "Livelihoods and Resources" for National Institute of Rural Development (NIRD), Hyderabad.

The journey continued and the engagement got augmented through work and discussions on various issues. It was more about respect for our souls and thoughts and the care for each other's family members. We have gone through many tough times in this divine journey but never ever ceased trying to do the virtuous. We went on to build a few assets (including knowledge) and did several activities by having a series of interactions with students, the community, and government officials, with the passing time, to enrich ourselves.

We had visited countless places together, in the last decade, to explore the finest work of legends and to appreciate the culture of our great history. We went on to understand the work of 'Art of Living foundation' in Bangalore during one of our visits, then to Pondicherry to visit Rishi Aurobindo's Ashram. We had been to the Buddhist heritage sites in

Sikkim and Bhutan, Jain Pilgrimage Center at Kolan Paka in Telangana and to a famous Sikh Gurudwara in Bidar in Karnataka. We felt different levels of energies for seeking eternal knowledge and wisdom. We started feeling perceptiveness and immense inspiration, soon after we got back from one famous and beautiful Shiva Temple; the temple was more than 1200 years old, near Kolan Paka in Telangana. As a hobby of seeking knowledge from history and the works of great people, we also visited several places of cultural and historical significance across India and a few places outside India. With this, we developed a similar approach to understand the world.

As a part of our spiritual journey, we learnt the value of yoga postures, pranayama, and meditation. The journey went on further and we started discussing writing something about the philosophy of a few great leaders and their spiritual views about life and their works. We started on some plain paper and with time constraints, things started taking shape unpredictably. We have dedicated significant amount of time to deliberate and re-discuss matters. We came across various ideas and thoughts which had facilitated us to shape our work, but not exactly the way we had envisioned it earlier, as if some external universal forces beckoned us to do something else.

We got enough time during lock down amid the COVID-19 pandemic, supported with our existing content base and experiences. Within 90 days, we have developed the content to capture the various knowledge and works in this comprehensive book, on the ideas of spirituality, sustainability, and about social interventions (3S) for a better world. We strongly feel these principles are more useful to this generation and to our next generation, to appreciate the good work done in the past and to appreciate the repository of ancient knowledge base across the globe, to feel the power within and to help the world to be prosperous and happy.

We have been inspired with the eternal journey which had started with a "big bang" as many people call it, for us to continue with love, respect and gratitude being a part of this creation by sharing good works and thoughts with the people of this world.

Best Wishes and Namaste

Introduction

This year, we applaud the 50th commemoration of Earth Day on April 22, 2020. Earth Day is celebrated to honour our planet earth, which has been nurturing us since the beginning of time. Everything in our lives comes from the Earth, 'The Good Earth.' The association that we have with nature is fundamental to our well-being. Destruction of biodiversity, global warming, climate change, leads to natural disasters with increased frequency and intensity; it also unleashes epidemics, poverty, conflict and violence against mankind, animals and nature, which are the main challenges that have dominated the first two decades of the 21st century. With the prevailing scenario, the world's social and common biophysical frameworks cannot sustain the aspirations of humanity.

Every country is in a mad race for economic growth even at the cost of the society. Human virtues are fast diminishing. Consumerism, dominance of technology companies, corporate greed, and emergence of global corporations as powerful empires, rising global inequality and egos of countries, are the emerging maladies across the globe. At any moment of time, the world with 7.8 billion population has 7.8 billion agendas. But now, amid COVID-19 pandemic, first time in the history of humanity, there is only one global agenda i.e., to survive. It has hit all societies, time zones and varying backgrounds over the globe. Global organisations and various research organisations are saying that more pandemics are yet to come.

Is nature giving us an exercise to re-evaluate what we have known as the truth, to alter our way of living and upgrade how we live, work and, associate with one another? Do we need a new world order? If yes, what should be the principles of the new world order?

Man needs to work on an approach that brings about sustainable production and consumption, respect for nature, individual values and ethics through value based education, bringing ethics in businesses with corporate social responsibility, integrity in media and government, leveraging ancient wisdoms backed by modern science, bringing inclusive innovations.

To address environmental issues and social challenges, ecological integrity, we must develop systems that protect our eco systems to prevent irreversible destruction. To safeguard our environment and our biosphere, man's inner self must evolve to foster sustainable development. The need of the hour is transition. Transition from the exploitative economic growth to inclusive and sustainable development and a happy society, respecting the inherent links between sustainability and spirituality is essential

Spirituality and ethics are vital components of human prosperity and process. What we need today is not technology revolution or economic revolution but the spiritual revolution. We need innovation with a guiding force of spirituality with the end result being socialism and sustainability.

The book throws light on the possible solutions to the present predicament that challenges humanity. It talks about ancient wisdom to overcome our maladies. It has seven parts with five to six chapters in each part. The first part talks about the purpose of life referring to the basic understanding of Who we are, Self-interest vs. Egoism, Sense of Belongingness and Oneness. In the second part, we have looked at life with the power of infinity and eternal truth from the perspective of Soul and Consciousness, Law of Cause and Effect, Power of Thoughts, Power of Love and Power of Prayer.

In the third part, we have deliberated on the fact that understanding the relationship between Science and Spirituality leads to Cosmic Realization: understanding the importance and power of cosmic energy and the means to receive it.

How can we have holistic health (physical, mental, and spiritual health) leveraging ancient and sacred Tools of well-being like yoga, regulated breathing, and meditation for day to day life and management.

The fourth part talks about the importance of sustainability for co-existence. This part highlights the negative impacts of consumption based economy, industrial agriculture system and the Dilemma of Economic Growth vs. Environment Protection, how to harness natural resources in a sustainable way, rediscovering traditional farming, role of business as a part of CSR to protect our planet and the need for paradigm shift from GDP based economic growth to happiness economy and a new economic order.

The fifth part talks about invisible challenges we are facing in terms of rising global inequality. In this part, we have discussed how data has become world's important resource and a controller of our lives, how the monopoly of corporations is controlling our food production system and the way of life, the big nexus between government and business and the way media controls how we think.

In the sixth part, we have discussed the importance of innovations to address social and environment challenges. How Innovations in both systemic innovations and frugal innovations can address the global challenges of climate change and sustainable use of energy for prosperity. We have also discussed how individual or the community can overcome harsh constraints and improvise an effective solution with limited resources.

The final and last part i.e. the seventh part talks about value-based education. How that ancient knowledge and wisdom can be blended with modern education system leading to prosperity of future generations. How Nature helps in enhancing creativity of students. How mentors and spiritual masters can guide us, and helps us achieve success much faster in life, be it in a corporate career or in personal development.

Part I

The Purpose

"Truth, purity, and
unselfishness —
wherever these are
present, there is no power
below or above
the sun to crush the
possessor thereof."

Swami Vivekananda

1

Who Am I & What Am I?

Who Am I?

Today, we busy ourselves trying to balance the various facets of our lives - the social, professional, and family life. And in that pursuit man has lost his touch with his own self. We are so judgmental of others that we become ignorant of the building blocks of our own character vis-à-vis our own nature. Centuries ago, Aristotle said, "Knowing yourself is the beginning of all wisdom" This is true even today. The 'Chinese philosopher and thinker Lao Tzu 614–517 BC' said "Knowing the world is knowledge; knowing oneself is wisdom".

To understand this, let us review the various prevalent concepts of the human being. Biologically, humans come under the animal kingdom with species name 'Homo Sapiens' whose forebrain or neo-cerebrum is more developed than that of other animals. Humans are not completely governed by animal instincts. Their drivers are self-controlled emotions, knowledge, and experiences.

According to medical science, the human being is a physiologically driven machine made up of complex biochemical molecules. Greek philosophers considered humans as rational animals. American philosopher "Benjamin Franklin" labelled humans, 'homo-faber' or a tool making animal. Karl max believed that the desire for economic gain is man's primary driver, and in his book "Das Kapital", defined humans as a social animal.

The famous aphorism "Know Thyself'" carved at the forecourt of the Delphian Apollo's temple in Greece is noteworthy. According to legends, Socrates is challenging us to know who we really are. Just how well do we really know ourselves? How do we answer the question: who am I?

Have we ever asked ourselves, 'Who am I really?' Am I Ram, a grandfather, a father, a husband, a friend, an artisan, a pilgrim, a pupil?

We may also identify ourselves in terms of relationships by responding to a call "father" because we have a child. A "husband" because we have a spouse. Many would identify themselves with their name, position, a designation, or a profession. We may also identify with the country where we live in, saying I am an Indian, I am a Tanzanian, I am Italian, I am Welsh and so on. There is a practice of identifying us with what we do at a given moment and the relationship at a given time. Hence, our identity, jobs, our wants, our belief that are dependent on factors, might change. We keep on creating new identities for ourselves, but the essence of who we are will never change.

So then, who are we? The answer to this question 'who am I' may not be known to us. The pursuit of carving out new identities for us creates a gap between this pursuer and our true self. There is a belief that all the turmoil and anxiety we experience is due to the ignorance of our true self. Till we recognize and acknowledge our true self, we might respond to the identity that has been assigned to us.

What Am I?

Am I this body? The body keeps changing. Body of a child and that of a youngster is not the same. Scientists have found that all the cells of a human body get replaced over a period. Medical science says that individual cells have a finite life span, and when they die off, they are replaced by new cells. According to "The New York Public Library's Science Desk Reference (Stonesong Press, 1995)" there are about 50 to

75 trillion cells in our body. Each category of cell has its own life span. The cells in our bodies live from a few hours, in the case of certain types of white blood cells, to a few weeks, for skin cells, to many decades, in the case of most brain cells. The bones you we have today are different from the bones we had a year ago. Therefore, we are not this body.

Am I this mind? Mind changes faster than body. Therefore, I cannot be the mind. So, what is the unchanging factor that I can identify with as this is what I am. So instead of asking 'who am I?', the ideal question should be what Am I. According to eastern philosophy (Yoga and Vedic philosophy) man is essentially a divine entity. You are an eternal Soul covered by various layers of body/sheath.

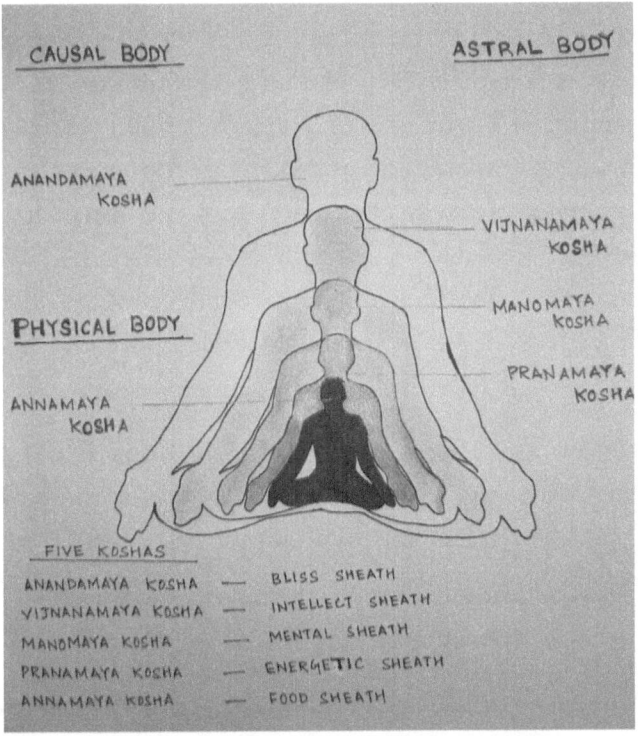

Adishankara, the 8th century Indian Philosopher and considered to the most one of the most authoritative Gurus of yoga and Vedic philosophy said that a living human being is made up of 3 bodies- a physical body or gross body, etheric body and an astral body. We can also say the body, mind, and the soul. Similarly, the Taittiriya Upanishad talks about five koshas (layers) of body which are also equated with the three bodies. These five koshas (sheaths) cover the Atman (soul).

Human body is the most efficient and best designed system that has ever been designed. The Physical or the gross body (Sthula sarira) has 5 elements namely earth, water, air, fire, and ether (space). Physical body (Sthula sarira) also called the Annamaya Kosha is the outer sheath made of muscles, bones, skin, and organs.

The second one is Subtle or Astral body (Sukshma sarira). This consists of the mind and the core energies that the body cannot do without to be alive. The Subtle body or the Astral body is composed of:

1. Pranamaya Kosha or the sheath of breath or energy. It oversees the breath and the flow of energy through the body.
2. Manomaya Kosha or Mind sheath is filled with the five kinds of sensory impressions. It deals with thoughts and emotions.
3. Vijnanamaya Kosha or Intellect sheath is also called knowledge sheath. This layer is comprised of wisdom, intuition, and perception. This helps us to take a decision on the choice of a life partner, or the brand of clothes to purchase etc.

The third one is the Causal body (Karana sarira), in which our experiences from the past are imprinted. This is referred to as the Anandamaya Kosha, the innermost sheath. This is the bliss sheath. It constitutes joy, love, peace, and total happiness.

Expanded View of Oneself

Vedic and Yogic philosophy answer three key questions, which allows us to understand that our sense of identity, is not permanent but temporal. Realization of this fact will further expand our view of ourselves. The questions surface from our innermost being. The questions are who am I? What do I want? How can I serve? As Swami Vivekananda said, "soul is potentially divine," Therefore, self-realization can lead to self-awareness.

How do we increase our self-awareness? As our concept of self gets clearer, self-awareness expands and our concern for others may increase simultaneously. Self-awareness not only helps one to progress spiritually, we may get a deeper inspiration to contribute to our community and our world.

Relationship Between Nature and Human Body

As per the yogic teachings and Vedanta philosophy, human body comprises of five elements namely earth, water, air, fire, and ether (space). Nature too is made up of five basic elements- earth, water, fire, air, and space. These elements embody the properties of nature. Everything that is solid in nature is Earth. Water is all things liquid. Everything gaseous is air. And fire is an element that transforms one state to another. For example, fire transforms the solid state of water (ice) into liquid water. Similarly, fire transforms liquid into its gaseous state (steam). Removal of fire begets the solid state. Expulsion of fire brings forth the solid state.

Chinese philosophers opine that all that there is in the universe corresponds to the five elements. Our body organs can be likewise connected to the five components. The five elements or five phases are classified by five materials as - wood, fire, earth, metal, and water. There is a strong relationship between both humans and nature.

Interestingly, the Ayurvedic system of Indian medicine and traditional Chinese medicine (TCM) known as five element acupuncture (FEA) have applied the five elements theory to clinical practice for healing purpose. We shall discuss about this later in this book.

Nature is imperative to man. Nature is independent. Once people gain proper understanding of man's connection with nature, they will live in harmony with nature and not oppose it, towards a journey of sustainable development.

2

Self-Interest vs. Egoism

What is the Source?

Over the years these words have gained a strong negative connotation. Let us first concentrate on Egoism. Once Oscar Wilde was asked to share the list of his 100 best books in the world, he said "I am afraid, that would be impossible to share. Then came the next question why? He said, "because I have written only five books". What does this statement reflect? Can we call this a classic case of an egoist?

The Upanishads clearly say that "self" is the source of all the problems of our daily lives. Selfish desires, cravings, attachments, hatred, and pride are traced to the sense of "I-ness" or ahamkara.

We are locked in the three sources of ego. The first one is that I am the Centre. The second one is being, my way is the best and third type is the egoistic sense of possessiveness.

The first one is the sense of the self. I am the center - It refers to the sense of self with a realization that we are individual entities, distinct from the environment around us. The seed of this feeling begins from infancy. For example, the parents, relatives paying attention to the slight discomfort of the infants. She/he likes to be the center of attention and with the lapse of time, develops a sense of self or ego, due to life experiences. I am the best. I am right. I know everything.

The second one is my way is the best. This feeling develops with one's own belief system. It is our expression of what we think is true. Beliefs can come from two sources: our own experience and reflections, or as an acceptance of ideas what other people, like family, teachers, religious leaders tell us. She/he does not hesitate to be aggressive and violent when his belief system is challenged.

The third one is the ego born out of possessiveness. Possessiveness generates from both object and people (one's wife, children, friends). When we express possessiveness, and we claim ownership over an object, this can lead to jealousy when others take an interest in our object. And that jealousy can lead to competitiveness arising from within us, to influence us to hold on to that which we claim as ours. And that jealousy and competitiveness can lead us to express anger and exercise control over whoever shows an interest in our object. That can lead to counter-productive thoughts, negative feelings, and unhelpful actions which disturb our peace and happiness. And in some cases, jealousy can have a domino effect that leads a person down a dark path that results in extreme reactions. Ego does not allow the external ideas to come in.

Osho has put plainly "Ego does not exist anywhere else except in human beings, and ego starts growing as the child grows. The parents, the schools, colleges, university, they all help to strengthen the ego for the simple reason that for centuries man had to struggle to survive and the idea has become a fixation, a deep unconscious conditioning, that only strong egos can survive in the struggle of life. Life has become just a struggle to survive. And scientists have made it even more convincing with the theory of the survival of the fittest. So, we help every child to become more and stronger in the ego, and it is there that the problem arises".

False Ego Versus Real Ego

According to Vedic literature (also Bhagavad-Gita), there are two types of ego. One is called as 'false ego' and other is 'real ego'. All the egos discussed above are false ego.

In Taittiriya Upanishads, a differentiation is drawn between a man's body and his soul. Man's body is not the real self. But deep within the man is the Atman or soul which is man's true self. Real identity or Real ego means identifying ourselves as 'soul' not the body. Brihad aranyak Upanishad says "अहं ब्रह्मस्मि". This means "I am not this body I am the soul". Interestingly, here we also find the involvement of I or Ego but the real ego...

Can We Escape from False Ego?

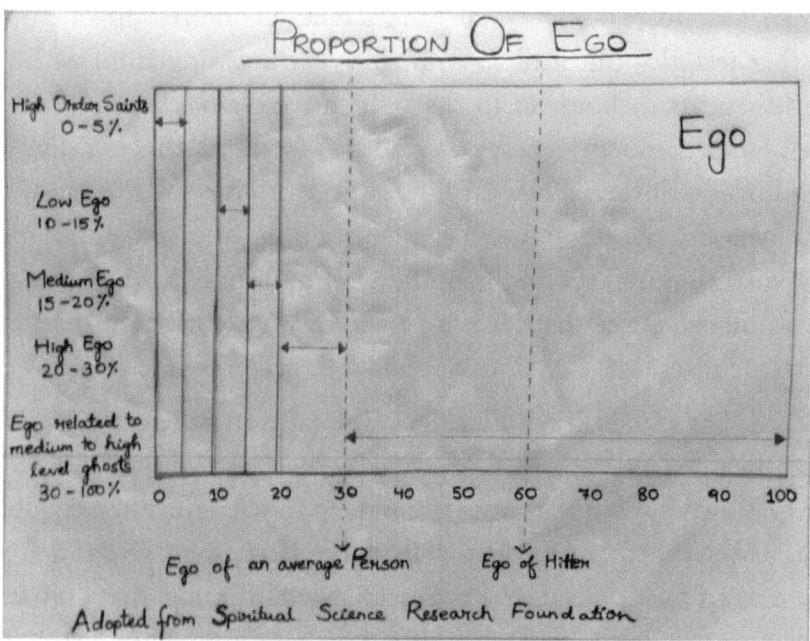

How do we escape from the false ego? Osho says-"The ego is a kind of absence. Because you do not know your true self, hence the ego. The moment you know your true self, no ego is found. Once we know the real self, the ego falls flat on the ground without any effort to surrender it. Unless the ego falls on its own, without your effort, it is not going to leave you". Reaching an ego-free state, whether brief or sustained, has been known as the stage of Illumination, Enlightenment, Nirvana, and Transcendence. We cannot escape completely from ego. However, we can reduce it through compassion, love, and surrender. Even the extremely evolved saints have some degree of ego. The degree of ego of a saint is less than the ego of an average person. Depending on the proportion, ego is classified as follows:

Can We Say That Egoism and Self-interest Are the Same?

Generally, self-interest motivates mankind. When we talk about self-interest, we remember Adam Smith, the economist known as the "father of modern economics". He clarifies that the best financial advantage for individual accrues from self-interest motivated actions. His clarification of the "theory of Invisible Hand" reveals that when large numbers of people act according to their own self-interest, goods and services are created that benefit both consumers and producers. Adam talks about this subject in his book 'The Wealth of Nations', explaining it this way: "It is not from the benevolence of the butcher, the brewer, or the baker that we expect our dinner, but from their regard to their own interest".

For example, in the stock market, it would be in your best interest if other investors feel optimistic and make a profit. In that way, the stock market will rise, thus resulting in more profit for you. Self-interest includes your ego and the surroundings as well. Therefore, we can say that self-interest is certainly a positive, progressive action that not only benefits the self but also its surroundings.

Prosperity of nations is a product of the liberal institutions when it allows people to run free their own individual self-interest. Self-interest drives ordinary human beings. Primarily, self-interest guides our urge to excel in life, our competitive attitude, our endeavour to fly high. The absence of self-interest would have rendered us incapacitated to upskill and upgrade ourselves.

Self Interest Versus Selfishness

There is a distinction between self-interest and selfishness. Selfishness is an over-obsessed attention to the self. All activities of an individual, his intentions, motives, ambitions head and heart are centred on his/her personal enrichment and personal well-being without any concern for society, country, and fellowmen. In other words, in selfishness, people try to minimise sacrifice and maximize incentive at the expense of others. Selfishness is not caring, acting negatively towards others but focusing on one's own gain. On the other hand, self-interest is not the conflict of interest with others in terms of not allowing others to grow.

In view of the aforesaid logic, if we can discard the selfish nature and use self-interest rationally, we can harmonize our interconnectivity with the universe and can achieve greater results for ourselves and the environment.

3

Sense of Belongingness

Accept Wisdom from Every Part of the World and Every Tradition

The need or sense of connection is inherent to man, but today society is almost devoid of community feeling. Media and other influencers lay emphasis on the differences that exist between one another and the gulf that divides us, instead of what unites us. So, it is up to us to bridge the gap and develop a connection through a sense of belonging and community feeling.

Currently in the globalised economy, there is a complete absence of multi-religious and multicultural education. We accept food from every part of the world. We eat Chinese food. It is not necessary to become Chinese to eat Chinese foods or become Swiss to eat Swiss chocolates. We also accept music and technology from every part of the world. Then, why can we not accept wisdom from every part of the world and every tradition? If we are given a little education and opportunity to learn about other religious and spiritual teachings and cultures, we would become broad minded and cherish a sense of belongingness with everybody around us in the world.

Let us quote few quotations on this from a few great personalities from different fields. "I am of the opinion that my life belongs to the community, and as long as I live it is my privilege to do for it whatever I can."- George Bernard Shaw. "I want Infosys to be a company which is globally respected and where in people belonging to different nationalities, races and religious beliefs will work with intense competition but utmost courtesy, dignity and co-operation in adding greater value to our stakeholders day after day"- N. R. Narayana Murthy. "We can never get a re-creation of community and heal our society without giving our citizens a sense of belonging."- Patch Adams

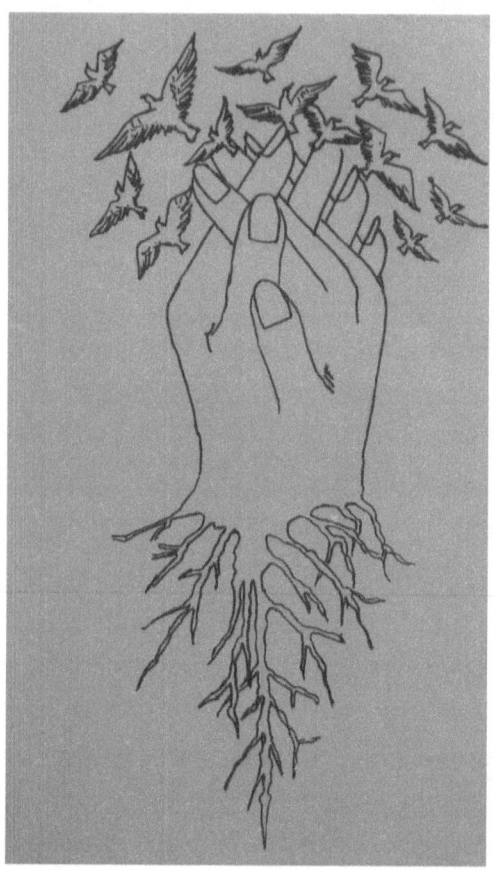

"We don't need bombs and guns to destroy, to bring peace - just get together, love one another, bring that peace, that joy, that strength of presence of each other in the home. And we will be able to overcome all the evil that is in the world" - Mother Teresa.

"We may have different religions, different languages, different coloured skin, but we all belong to one human race."- Kofi Annan

We Are All One, Without Any Distinction of Nation, Race, Color and Faith

To imbibe this philosophy in our life, we need to have a deep understanding and experience that we are all one—all manifestations of the same Consciousness. For instance, Christianity says we all come from God, and are the children of God; so, we are all brothers. In such a case we would not hurt one another.

Similarly, Advaita Vedanta teaches that universe is nothing but Pure Consciousness. Everything emanates from nature made of the same substance. That separation is a wrong notion. Many great thinkers have repeatedly invoked the idea of one. Narayana Guru imagined a casteless society or a society of only one 'caste', what he called the "Manusha Jati". There have been countless thinkers who have called for 'one humanity' as the ideal that we should follow.

Oneness would prevent wars, exploitation, injustice, violence, abuse, and environmental damage, among other problems. Understanding this phenomenon and experiencing its synchronicity is the foundation of oneness religion or oneness spirituality.

In present day times, the Declaration of Human Rights by UNO announces in its article 2 that every single person is qualified for the rights recorded in the charter without the differentiation of race, sex, and language and so on.

Guru Nanak's Message on Oneness- A Light for Humanity

The concept of Oneness seems to be missing from various facets of our life. When we talk of oneness, it reminds us of Guru Nanak's message of "Ik Onkar" or eternal message of oneness, that we are all one, without any distinction of nation, race, colour, caste, and faith.

In the context of caste, the Guru highlighted the oneness of castes by refusing to wear the sacred thread. On gender, he advocated equality for women. (Women give birth to Kings, so they are equivalent to Kings). He said that "it is the woman who gives birth to a man; it is she who makes the kings and other great men". Without her, man is incomplete. Respecting this truth, the Sikh Gurus invited woman to join the "Sangat" (congregation), work alongside men in the "Langar" (common Kitchen), and be participators in all the religious, social, and cultural activities of the Gurdwaras (Sikh places of worship). Many examples are seen in Sikh history that show that the women worked and cooperated with men, at times with a greater vigour. Mata Gujri (the mother of Guru Gobind Singh) and Mata Sundri are worth mentioning. Mata Sundri led the community during important time immediately after the death of her husband Guru Gobind Singh.

On oneness on the economic scale, he criticised kings for levying heavy taxes on their subjects. He also spoke about man's oneness with nature, when he said, "Pavan guru, pani pita, mata dharat mahat'. In the context of cosmic oneness, he said the cosmos is in a constant state of 'arti' where the sun and the moon are the lamps. He said that every minute of our life is an arti, sacred offering to the Lord. Since we are all part of the same creator, we should practice oneness in all walks of life for a peaceful society.

4

Vasudhaiva Kutumbakam

The Whole Earth is Just One Family

The phrase "Vasudhaiva Kutumbakam" (Sanskrit word: वसुधैव कुटुम्बकम्) consists of three Sanskrit words namely Vasudha, Aiva and Kutumbakam. The meaning of Vasudha is the earth, Aiva denotes emphasizing and Kutumbakam stands for family. These three words convey the truth that the entire earth is a family thereby promoting global citizenship. This philosophical concept nurtures humanity as one family.

Humans are 99.9% identical in terms of generic makeup. Of course, each human being is unique in terms of his genetic makeup. What makes us unique is the difference of only 0.1% of our genome. So, this supports the idea of one world family that essentially, we are all same.

Single life energy is at the core of human existence that emanates from the Creator. Consider the ocean as one body, how can a droplet from the ocean have a different identity? Obviously, both have the same characteristics, or else how will it dissolve in the ocean. Chapter 6 of the Maha Upanishad and the Rig Veda have the original phrase. This is the overriding moral value of the Indian society. So, at the entrance hall of the Indian parliament this verse is sculpted.

अयं बन्धुरयंनेति गणना लघुचेतसाम् उदारचरितानां तु वसुधैव कुटुम्बकम् ॥

Universal brotherhood is a concept of equality of all humans. They are equal irrespective of their caste, creed, race, religion, gender and so on. The world is one big family. We are interdependent for numerous reasons. It supports universal love and peace for the whole human race. Humanity is engulfed in Universal Consciousness and it is in us.

It is common knowledge that our world in a global village. Global recession, destruction of biodiversity, climate change, overheating of the atmosphere, poverty, wars, and epidemics are huge problems that humanity is facing in the first two decades of the 21st century.

Different countries with their economic and military power are competing to secure their interests even at the risk of trampling over common global values including environment protection. The 21st century has an immediate and great necessity to imbibe the Indian philosophy of 'Vasudhaiva Kutumbakam' for peaceful co-existence and creating an age of peace, affluence, and contentment on the earth.

It may not be out of place to mention here that the principle of reciprocity is to be kept in mind to apply this philosophy. To illustrate, we can emulate reciprocation from the history of India: take an example of reciprocity from Indian history: When the Parsi people were extended shelter in India, they continued to live on this soil, and were eternally grateful for this benevolence. One interesting Parsi legend is about the initial meeting of the just-landed Parsi immigrants on the coast of Gujarat and the local king of Gujarat, Jadi Rana. Zoroastrians requested asylum, to which king Jadi Rana pointed to a pot filled to the very brim with milk, to convey to them that that his kingdom was populated enough and expressed his inability to accept refugees. A Zoroastrian priest from that group, proceeded to add a pinch of sugar to the pot of milk to signify that their community would sweeten the pot of milk, without spilling/displacing any milk. Jadi Rana wholeheartedly gave shelter to the immigrants and allowed them to practice their religion and traditions freely. Parsis continue to enrich/sweeten the lives of Indians. Great many people in the fields of science, technology, art, business, and sports have sprung from among those Parsis who were welcomed on Indian shores.

Let us give another example. During the Second World War, Poland was reeling under destruction and devastation, with their people being cast into concentration camps and children being orphaned. Under duress, many women and children escaped via the sea route, only to be turned away by several countries when they sought refuge. On their ship's approach to the Indian shores, the British governor in Mumbai refused them entry. Maharaja Digvijaysinhji Ranjitsinhji Jadeja of Jamnagar on hearing about this, intervened on their behalf, with the British Governor General, only to be turned down. His intervention unsuccessful, he graciously came forward and gave his permission to allow the ship to dockat Rosi port in his province. Thus, began the story of Little Poland in India. The Maharaja "Jam Saheb Digvijay Singh", gave shelter to 500 women and their children, in addition, free education to the children in Balachiri, an army school. These Polish people lived in Jamnagar for nine years. One of the refugee children later became the Prime Minister of Poland. Poland has many roads in Warsaw named after Maharaja Jam Sahib; many schemes are named after the Maharaja. Every year Polish newspapers print articles about benevolence of Maharaja Jam Saheb Digvijay Singh.

The Bene Israel who, descent of the "lost" ten tribes of Israel, were exiled from their capital, Samaria, by the Assyrian King Shalmaneser and subsequent kings from the year 722 AD onward. It is believed that these tribes on being shipwrecked were washed ashore on the Konkan coast, south of Bombay. The locals gave them shelter among their lands and they settled permanently on the Konkan shores.

The spiritual leader Dalai Lama says "The whole of humanity is one human family. This planet is our only home". A new vision must come forth from the leaders of society, the youth, religions, and educational institutions. We need to think of our earth as the family and do combined work to build peace and harmony among communities, and nations. Further there is a need for developing and implementing common norms to address contentious issues of the world ranging from climate changes, health, and food security issues.

You Can Live Happily Anywhere

It reminds us the famous quote of Marcus Aurelius "Let it be clear to you that the pace of green fields can always be yours, in this, that or any other spot; and that nothing is any different here from what it would be either up in the hills, or down by the sea, or wherever else you will."

The cause of a lot of misery comes from the view that the "grass is greener on the other side of the field". We see what we do not have/possess and crave that despite having enough to live comfortably and happily. If we live in a suburb, we wish our home were in the countryside or on the beach and vice versa.

5

Attachment with Detachment

Root Cause of Sorrow

When an individual comes to this life, he comes alone, bare-handed but when he goes back, he carries a big bundle of attachments. The attachment can be towards ones dear and near ones, attachment to his/her possessions and attachment towards many attractions of the world. Attachment is when we are either physically, intellectually, or emotionally bound to something dearly.

The deeper the attachment, deeper is the binding. According to the Bhagvad Gita attachment is the root cause of sorrow. Buddhism too states that the root cause of misery is attachment. Gautam Buddha said, "Attachment leads to Suffering". Let us try and understand what exactly we mean by attachment. The clear definition of attachment is very important. Attachment is when we hold something very precious to us, so much so, that we may not be willing to part with it. If you are extremely attached to our wife, will you be willing to part with her? Of course not. If she were to die in your lifetime, your deep attachment to her will send you into a deep state of shock. A deep attachment to something makes its loss a very deep sorrow. Let us take another example. There are people who occupy positions of great power. They suddenly become attached to their power. The power they have, becomes an intoxicant to them. They cannot imagine their lives without it.

Now let us imagine that in the normal ups and downs of the world, they were to lose their power, what would they feel? They would be absolutely hostile. They will not be able to come to terms with the loss of their power. Therefore, when such power-hungry people are enjoying power, they will do even the cruellest of acts to hold on to their power. The cruellest dictators in the world who have killed thousands to hold on to their power belong to this category.

Attachment is fatal. The deeper, the deadlier. We are often so attached to some of our important relationships. Some friendships are very dear to us. We have a very deep attachment to those friends. Suddenly, due to some misunderstanding what would happen if that friendship were to break? Indeed, we would be terribly heartbroken. We would be experiencing deep pain and misery.

Seven Deadly Attachments

Let us in short see what kind of deep attachments should be avoided. There are seven deadly attachments. These are Relationships, Life, Wealth, Power, Fame, Possessions and Self.

The first attachment is relationship. If we are too attached to our relationships, then any loss of the same can leave us mentally distraught. Relationships must be viewed as a special boon and bonus and not our birth right. Enjoy the love and warmth in them. But always remember that we are a guest in this world and so are all our relationships.

The second one is life. If we are attached to life, how will we embrace death when it comes? We will violently resist the call of death. We need to view life as temporary. The more often we remember death, the less we become attached to life. Ancient wisdom tells us that wise men often remember death. This induces humility, contentment, and gratitude in them. In the context of humility, chapter 18 V 53 of Bhagvad-Gita mentions "Let him (a wise man) give up all thought of 'I', force, pride"

The third one is wealth. If we are attached to our wealth, any financial loss will leave us in mental disaster. Wealth is a material possession. Why value the material? The real value is in our values. We should be attached to values and not to wealth. We should be afraid to lose values.

The fourth one is power. If we are attached to power, then we will stoop to the lowest level to hold on to it. We cannot accept the loss of power. our values will be destroyed to satisfy our greed and attachment for power. It will create a useless human being in us.

The fifth one is fame. If we are attached to fame, we will do anything to be in the public eye. The glory of our name means much to us. We may destroy all other names, even God's, so that our name becomes glorious.

The sixth one is possessions. If we are attached to our possessions, then we will guard every possession of ours like a miser. We will never give a thing to others. We will hoard everything. And when we lose our possessions, it will bring us grief.

The seventh one is self. If we are attached to our self, we will not be willing to merge into the larger universal self. The 'I' in our self and ego will prevent this merging. We will remain attached to ourselves and smallness. How sad is this!

Can We Detach from Attachment?

Everyone deep inside knows that attachment leads to suffering. It just needs to be re-discovered. We need to be aware those 7 deadly attachments mentioned above and bring in the detachment key.

Detachment does not mean lack of love. Detachment does not mean lack of feeling or emotion. In fact, in detachment we can reach the deepest emotional depths. This is because we have a trump card that we are not afraid to lose. Our love can be far deeper than someone whose love comes with attachment. Attached love always is in fear of losing itself. Therefore, it is wise to be cautious at every step and avoid all risks to ensure that it does not lose the object of its love. Hence, it cannot go deeper. Its expression is severely hindered. In a free, fearless love which is not bound by attachment, the emotional depth can go very, very deep. This type of love has true meaning, true feeling, true depth. It truly enjoys every moment of its emotional experience with total freedom without fear.

The Bhagavad Gita has wonderfully explained the concept of detachment. Krishna tells Arjuna that "acting with detachment means doing the right thing for its own sake, because it needs to be done, without worrying about success or failure".

All attachments are just that way. They bind us, make us fearful. They rob us of our true freedom. We become caged within our attachments. Life needs to be viewed with the prism of temporariness. Nothing is permanent. So, enjoy every moment of this short experience without ever being attached to even a single memory or material. We were only a guest in this world. Do not start imagining permanence to our earthly existence. That is the cause of our pain and sorrow. It is called attachment. When attached to persons or properties, the world appears very attractive for the individual. The individual therefore wants to remain in this world for as long as possible. Even when the time for departure comes and the inevitable death occurs, he leaves the world reluctantly.

According to Vivekananda- Attachment gives us pleasure. Closeness to our friends, family, intellect, and spirituality brings us joy. We get close to material objects in the world which proves that sadness is sure to follow due to this closeness. If we can separate ourselves from all matters of the material world, we would be less miserable or free of misery.

Swami Vivekananda further says, "There are 'The Walls' the ones who never get attracted by anything. They do not suffer from misery but can never love or be loved. Next are 'The Attached', the ones who are completely attached to the work they are doing and hence to the result of the work. These people get work done but are caught in the vicious cycle of karma and face huge problems when departing from the object of attachment. Superior to these are the ones who are detached, who work with full force and can attach themselves and detach themselves at will. These are what can be called the 'The Detached'. These are the ones that understand the nature of work, get most work done and get most of what god has to offer via work"

Detaching from external things does not mean that we get rid of them. Detachment has nothing to do with indifference or carelessness. We just let it go. We simply comprehend that it is not things or other people that can really make us happy in a reliable way. That leads to a natural state of letting go. We see that we alone are responsible for our well-being – not things and people around us. Through letting go, we become freer and more relaxed. Not operating from a state of perceived lack or fear we are free to live our life with ease. For example, in our relationships, we can give our best and do our best. So, our attachment to them is complete. However, we remain detached in the sense that we do not expect them to reciprocate our affection.

6

Forget & Forgive

Breaking Karmic Chains

Forgiveness refers to letting go of the past grudges or anger against a person. Past grudges and desire for revenge wreak havoc on our life, our mind, and our soul. We drag this heavy ball and chain around everywhere we go, preventing any forward growth. When we hold onto negative emotions, we give our power away to the one who has hurt us, allowing our subconscious mind to take control of our life. Keeping us locked in a repetitive cycle of victimhood until we are ready to let go of the pain. We bury a great deal of hurt and pain deep within our subconscious minds. Since we do not remember them, we believe we are free of them. This is not so! This hurt and pain are an energetic memory stored within our subconscious mind. It runs our lives! It is a programme that keeps replaying over and over and fools us into believing we are a victim.

Hence Forgiveness is a prescription for breaking those karmic chains that have been wound around us for many lifetimes. Forgive them, take back your power, rid yourself of this negative energy and move on with love and peace in our life! We must ease all negative karmic energy that we have together in all of time. In other words, forgiveness frees us from our debt of bad karma by escaping from the wheel of negativity.

Forgiveness is a virtue, and when we forgive others, we come to terms with the sadness experienced by us by their bad intent. The Bhagavad-Gita teaches us that forgiveness is a part of the goodness, in our journey of reaching our goal of enlightenment. Arjuna time and again begged forgiveness of Lord Krishna for the way he behaved, for questioning the Lord, doubting him, his ignorance, and the inability to judge. Lord Krishna repeatedly with love and benevolence because the Gita says that one can repent and ask for forgiveness, for faults committed with intent or without intent.

Essential Aspect of Divine Grace

When one is in a higher state of mind, forgiveness comes easily. It is a very spiritual state of being and something that needs to be practiced for receiving spiritual blessings. A lot of efforts need to be made in the moral field and one needs to be devoted to the higher being. Superior entities like intelligence, knowledge, truthfulness, control of the senses, control of the mind, fearlessness, nonviolence, austerity, and charity must be a part of your life to attain that sacred grace. When Jesus was being crucified on the cross, amid pain, suffering and humiliation, Jesus asked his father to forgive those who were killing him! What greater example of forgiveness can there be! It is very important to mention the forgiveness day observed by the followers of Jainism.

"Forgiveness Day" is a day of forgiving and seeking forgiveness that the followers of Jainism observe. On the last day of the annual "Paryushana festival", all Jains follow the practice of reaching out to everyone, to seek their forgiveness for all the faults/mistakes made by them knowingly or unwittingly. Mahavira said "We should forgive our own soul first. To forgive others is a practical application of this supreme forgiveness. All souls are equal and similar and have the same nature and qualities".

Greatest Examples of Forgiveness in the Modern World

Nelson Mandela's name is synonymous with forgiveness. Mandela said that "Forgiveness liberates the soul, it removes fear. That's why it's such a powerful weapon." His lifestyle of reconciliation, love and forgiveness is worth mentioning. Instead of revenge and retribution, he chose to forgive and made peace with his captors and jailors; those who engaged in terrible atrocities against the non-white population in South Africa. Mandela was showered many honours, including the Nobel Peace Prize in 1993 impeccable forgiving lifestyle. Mandela's lifestyle of forgiveness is an example to the entire human race.

During our visit to South Africa on a consulting assignment for the government of South Africa in the year 2017, we arrived in Cape Town on a Sunday morning. Since it was a Sunday, as a part of local site seeing, the first stop of our visit was Robben Island prison, the infamous prison where Nelson Mandela and other leaders of black liberation movement were held in captivity for decades during apartheid regime. Now after the abolition of apartheid and the formation of African National Congress (ANC) under the leadership of Nelson Mandela coming into power, this prison has become a tourist spot. A long-term prisoner formed a trust to operate Robben Island as a tourist destination and they served as a guide as well. Interestingly, many of the ex-prisoners have become tourist guides. While interacting with the tourist guide, we came to know that many of the ex-jailers are still living on the Island. Now ex-prisoners have become guides and some of the ex-jailors are employed by the very prisoners as guides. The ex-prisoners are living serenely with ex-jailors with no sign of hatred for the jailors. We would say this is a classic example of "forget the past and get on the future" attitude or an attitude of forgiveness. During our travel to other places like Pretoria and Johannesburg, we found the same attitude prevailing among most of the South Africans.

It is also worth mentioning forgiveness by Mahatma Gandhi of Brigadier General Dyer, the chief perpetrator of the Jallianwala Bagh massacre. General Dyer was hated by Indians, but Mahatma Gandhi chose to forgive General Dyer repeatedly, even as he warned people against 'Dyerism'. Gandhi said that "it would be a sin for me to serve General Dyer and co-operate with him to shoot innocent men. But it will be an exercise of forgiveness or love for me to nurse him back to life if he was suffering from a physical malady"

Part II

Feeling the Infinity

"Your trials did not come
to punish you, but to
awaken you – to make
you realise that you are
a part of Spirit and that
just behind the sparks
of your life is the Flame
of Infinity"

Paramahansa Yogananda

7

Soul & Consciousness

Does Our 'Self' Have a Soul?

To understand soul, let us try to understand the concept of "Dualism". The belief that reality or the existence of humanity is in two parts, is Dualism. The identity of the two parts is the body and the soul.

The Bhagavad-Gita tells us that the soul is, "invisible and inconceivable… unbreakable, insoluble, and can be neither be burned nor dried". It continues, "For the soul, there is neither birth nor death at any time. The soul is unborn, eternal, and ever existing. The soul is not slain when the body is slain. Upanishads say that the soul is one ten-thousandth the size of the tip of hair. Without the soul, the body is just a lifeless lump of matter that starts decaying and loses all its attractiveness.

We have to admit that no matter how close we are to someone, once the soul leaves the body, we would prefer not to hang around the body for long. Upanishads also explain that the soul resides in the region of the heart. If someone gets a heart transplant, are they also getting a new soul?" No. The soul is believed to be in the region of the heart and does not get dislodged when the heart is removed. The "real person" is residing within the body. The body is often compared to a vehicle, while the soul is the driver. A vehicle will not function without the driver. The soul resides in the vehicle made not of metal, but of flesh and bones. The eyes then become the headlights and the limbs become akin to the wheels which allow movement.

To search further on the concept of soul, let us look at the views of ancient scholars like Socrates, Plato, and Augustine. Socrates believed the soul is everlasting. He declared with death; existence does not come to an end. It is something that helps raise the soul from the physical body. Plato was convinced that the soul is eternal and therefore detached from the body. He believed that the soul lives in the body until life gets extinguished. That soul moves to another body. Therefore, Plato termed the body "the prison of the soul." It sounds more like re-incarnation or cycle of birth and death. Augustine also believed that soul is immortal. The soul and the body make up the human. He believed that one soul and one body make up one person. He did not buy into the idea that it hops from one body to anther body.

Dr Wilder Penfield wanted to prove wrong, the existence of the soul, when he started his brain research. He experimented with people on their brains by sending electrical pulses, making them raise arms, vocalize, and recall memories involuntarily, but he discovered he could not stimulate the will. In 1950, Dr Penfield declared in his book, "The Mystery of the Mind has clearly articulated that the brain is a computer, but it is programmed by something outside of itself." This something is nothing but the soul.

Human Consciousness- Spiritual Spark of Soul

The soul is nothing but the inner flicker of light which makes us aware that we are conscious. The Bhagavad-Gita tells us that "something outside of itself" is the soul, or we can call this our "conscience", which is nothing but the "inner voice", the soul.

We can define human consciousness as a capacity to be aware, perceive, experience, and feel sensations such as pain and suffering, or pleasure and comfort. We know very little about how consciousness works, although it plays a very important role in our lives. Example of Human Consciousness can be the possibility for us to sense the suffering of others and to respond with helping acts.

Scientists and philosophers agree that the brain does not produce consciousness, but it act as a kind of a receiver which "picks up" the fundamental consciousness that is all around us, and "transmits" it into our own being. Our thoughts, feelings, words, and actions determine our level of consciousness.

How to Elevate Our Consciousness

Now, we may wonder if we can take our consciousness to a higher level. Well, the answer is yes. We can elevate our consciousness to a higher level. This can happen when we believe and then see. Believe it or not, the phenomenon of movement of consciousness between two or more levels of conscious awareness occurs frequently in our daily lives depending on our circumstances.

We can reach a higher level of conscious thought if we learn to master our thoughts and emotions and adopt the finer aspects like sympathy, empathy, goodwill, tolerance, appreciation, supreme love, patience, modesty, truthfulness, and forbearance etc. We can elevate our conscious thoughts via meditation and other sacred principles, that include mindfulness and heartfulness and follow the teachings of ancient spiritual masters.

The greatest gift we can give to the world is elevating our consciousness. What we need today in this world are more people with higher consciousness level. We may strive for increasing our level of consciousness and co-create a happy and peaceful world.

David Hawkins in his book Power vs Force has talked about the range of human consciousness. He deliberated on the different range of awareness that human beings experience. It goes from "Shame" to "Enlightenment". The readings that range between 1 and 1000 representing the strength of all types of human awareness. The readings were finetuned via millions of "kinesiological" trials, often referred to as "muscle testing", on scores of people spanning 20 years. He found the strength of a limited people with high consciousness equalizes the weak consciousness of a whole lot of people at the base of the spectrum. When the book was written in 1992, it was found that around 15 percent of total world's humanity possessed the level of consciousness score of just above 200 (critical consciousness level), considered necessary. This percentage could equalize the below-positive consciousness of the remaining 85 percent. The "kinesiological" testing has shown that one candidate of level 700 can counter the balance brought along by 70 million people of scores of below 200. In the same way, 1 human being with a level of 600 can balance out ten million with less than 200.

My Life is in Harmony with the Universe

We get struck to shallow consciousness due to the sense we feel of being alone, apart from, and not in tune with others. We believe we are separate from everything else, alone, and vulnerable.

The following Sanskrit phrases remind us that we are in a grand collaboration with the universe. "Aham Brahmasmi" ~ I am the universe, "Om Vardhanam Namah" ~ The universe and I, nourish each other. "Om Varunam Namah" ~ My life and the universe and in perfect harmony. Our personal body is not separate from the body of the universe. This is well explained in "Chandogya Upanishad" which sates "Tat Tvam Asi" (तत्त्वमसि) This is also translated as "I am that, you are that, all this is that. In other words, personal body and the body of the universe are not separate from each other.

Try and stop perceiving yourself as "separate." The feeling would be something very different. How differently we would feel. There would be scope for us to exhibit patience, kindness and compassion to everyone around us.

8

Law of Karma or Cause and Effect

My Actions Are Aligned with Cosmic Law

We have heard of the Karmic law, in other words, using science, we call it the "cause and effect" law. The underlying meaning remains the same.

Unlike the pure science laws, the karmic law follows a different path: the highest of psychological or the "Godly" laws. If we were to equate it to Newton's "third law of motion", that explains the interplay of physical objects whereas the Karmic law looks at all deeds that human beings commit helps balance the correlation among the living humanity.

According to the basic Sanskrit definition, karma simply means "action." "The law of Karma" is the greatest of laws: "cause and effect", of "action and reaction", that determines the outcome of all living beings. Essentially, whatever deeds we do, starts an energy that returns to us, in some manner. In other words, action and reaction are equal and opposite. When we cause sadness to others, the karmic law, sees to it that the same kind of sadness must be experienced by us for sure, whether in this life or the afterlife.

The Bhagavad Gita enlightens us on the importance of action as Karma yoga. People who live in the society and have saintly attitude to do good to humanity and to the world, with their noble action, are known as Karma Yogi.

Karma is universal law found in all religions, philosophies, and sciences. Do you remember the Biblical saying? "A man reaps what he sows" The same saying has its expression in other religions as well. Judaism says, "What is hateful to you, do not do to your fellow: this is the whole Torah; the rest is the explanation; go and learn." Zoroastrianism says, "Do not do unto others whatever is injurious to yourself". Confucius says "One word which sums up the basis of all good conduct…loving-kindness. Do not do to others what you do not want done to yourself". Buddhism teaches "Treat not others in ways that we, ourselves, would find hurtful". Christianity says, "So in everything, do to others what you would have them do to you, for this sums up the Law and the Prophets." Buddha also says "When a bird is alive, it eats ants. When the bird is dead, ants eat the bird. One tree makes a million match sticks. Only one matchstick is needed to burn a million trees. Time and Circumstance can change at any moment. Do not devalue or hurt anyone in life. We may be powerful this time but remember: Time is more powerful than us. So be good and do good"

To explain the law of cause and effect, the way climate change is affecting world economy and the socioeconomic balance, is a good example. There is a consensus among Climate scientists that human violence unleashed on nature causes global warming that results in climate change.

Decision Choices and Consequences

Karma is the godly version of the scientific "law of cause and effect" which makes our thoughts, words and actions find their way back to their origin (us) sooner or later. In other words, our current life, effect, is the result of a particular "cause". Causes, are our decisions that are made on an ongoing basis. It is not relevant if these decisions of ours vary in their simplicity or significance.

Every decision that we as human beings have made, from as far back as, when we could make them, has had particular effect on our lives. Therefore, we should be fully aware and be conscious while making choices of decisions every moment. To live in the present moment and be conscious of this, helps us to make conscious decisions. At the decision making moment, our thoughts pass through two question-gates: "What are the consequences of this decision choice that we are making?" and "Is it going to make me a better person, make me happy, as well as those affected by my decision".

"Law of Compensation"- Redefining The Law of Karma

"The Law of Compensation" is restatement of the law of cause and effect. The tiny seed must struggle to break the hard earth, to come forth, and when it is welcomed by sunshine and the right nutrients, grows into a tree (effect). The tree turns out as per the law of compensation. This natural law which compensates, is all pervasive, if we are watchful. For the desert heat of Rajasthan area, freezing cold pervades in Kashmir. Compensation is everywhere in nature. Just as there are antisocial elements in a society, we find a handful of spiritual and godlike individuals, to counter the ill effects caused by the first lot.

The changing climate is a worrying scenario that humanity faces. This law of compensation is applicable in Climate change also. The "National Plan on Climate Change report", sees a pattern of increasing monsoon rains in the west coast, northern parts of Andhra Pradesh, NW India (an increase between 10 and 12 percent, on the regular rains in the last decade). While, a declining monsoon is being experienced in eastern Madhya Pradesh, NE India, as well as in Gujarat and Kerala in the last decade.

"The law of compensation" is evidenced in the intellectual area as well. An action of ill intent attracts an equal and opposite result, as if to justify. Likewise, a mind full of good thoughts, ideas, good plans for betterment, contentment, and positive thoughts, will yield similarly good resultant experiences in our life.

Karma Types- Learning from Mahabharata

According to the learnings from Mahabharata, Karma can be classified into three types. Kriyamana Karma, Sanchita Karma, and Prarabdha Karma. It can be explained through the lesson of Karma from Mahabharata.

Dritarashtra and Gandhari were among the unfortunate and had lost all their 100 sons. After hearing about the death of their beloved son Duryodhan, Gandhari collapsed out of shock and grief. King Dritarashtra bowed down before Lord Krishna and prayed. "Oh Lord! There cannot be anyone in this world who is as unfortunate as me. I was born blind; I never saw my children's faces and I do not know what they looked like. I never did anything wrong in my life, I was limited by blindness. Why did I still have to go through this terrible punishment? What wrong did I do?"

Lord Krishna then explained the laws of Karma to Dritarashtra. Karma means actions that we perform on a day to day basis. From the time we are born every minute we are doing some actions or Karma. He also explained the three types of karmas.

Kriyamana Karma means the actions that we perform every minute & every seconds. The effect of this Karma is experienced within a few days or within our present lifetime. The remaining Karma may stay and get accumulated. It waits of an opportune time to affect us. This Karma that gets accumulated is called Sanchita Karma. The opportune time for accumulated Karma can come within one lifetime or may come after several rebirths. "Prarabdha Karma" is an extension of "Sanchita Karma", a record of our past deeds, that waits to be completed by one's experience in the current body or via incarnation.

Lord Krishna then granted Dhritarashtra the divine vision to look back into his previous births. Dhritrashtra discovered that 50 births back he was a ruthless hunter and once, just to have some fun, he threw a burning net on a tree full of birds. Thus, causing 100 fledglings to perish. Despite being able to escape, the surviving birds were blinded by the extreme heat caused by this fire. Because of Sanchita Karma he was destined to remain blind in this Life and lose his 100 sons.

After listening to Krishna's enlightened explanation, Dhritrashtra inquired "Krishna why did I not get punished in that birth itself, or the next birth, for the great sin that I had committed? Why now?". Lord Krishna smiled and replied "Your Karma had to wait for an opportune time for 50 Births. During which time you could earn and accumulate enough pious deeds to attain the merit of being born a king and have 100 sons in one lifetime. The Sanchita Karma accumulated over the last 50 births would influence your life as Prarabdha Karma and could then instantaneously confront you with the effects of that evil action."

How to Attract Good Karma?

There are 5 key approaches to attract good karma. The first one is forgiveness. Forgiveness is a very powerful action that helps a person to be rid of the heavy burden of the guilt or wrongs, he carries within him.

The second one is making conscious choices. Before taking any decision, we must pause and ponder over why, what and the how of the decision or choice we are going to make; and how it might affect ourselves and those around us, that matter. It is a good practice to pay attention to our heart as well as that inner voice that helps you with the knowledge of right and wrong. One of the worst battles we will have to fight is the one between what we know in our head and what we feel in our heart. Swami Vivekananda once said, "In a conflict between the heart and the brain, follow your heart".

The third one is cleansing our self of the unnecessary and useless waste material piling up in our mind, body, and space, as well as time. We can detoxify our body and mind several times annually, if required, by making a change in our location and situation. These steps go a long way to unblock any blockage and to remove bad vibes.

The fourth one is spread good vibration. It is possible to send soft and healing suggestions of love and wellbeing to anyone and everyone as we go through our business of living. This can cover plants and animals we encounter or otherwise. In case, we happen to see or meet someone/something that we are not happy with or at peace with, there is even more reason to send out positive vibration of love and healing their way. After all, we are all encompassed and interconnected in this one Universe.

The fifth one is devotion to divine. Connecting with God is the most vital aspect of this journey. Exercising gratitude every moment of every living timespan, helps us develop a need for being of service. Living gratitude and practicing service, spreading a ripple effect of good, peace and harmony, helps us to attain good karma through our connection with the almighty.

9

Power of Thoughts

Thought-Process Driving Every Life Event to Create History of the World

Thoughts have been the root cause of the humanity's problems. War is the resultant evil that had its root in the thoughts of someone somewhere, to begin with. Murder was hatched in a tiny thought, in someone's troubled mind. Rape is a thought problem. Even climate change is a thought problem because it is based upon greed which is a thought problem.

Thoughts can be equated to giants, the humungous dinosaurs in terms of power. They loom larger than the power of electricity. Dictate our life, mould our character, and shape our destiny. A cascade of very strong and power filled thoughts are behind every great event in life and in the history of the world. Behind all philosophies, discoveries, and inventions, behind all lifesaving or life-destroying devices are thought first.

Once the thought is acknowledged, most people, they focus their energy on that something, through action and start working towards it. If our action is strong enough, our thought becomes a reality. That is the usual way we function in the world. But we do not know how to infuse or empower that thought with a certain dimension of energy.

Let us quote from Rigveda which says आ नो भद्राः क्रतवो यन्तु विश्वतः Aano bhadra krtavo yantu vishwatah"(1.89.1 Rigveda. This means "Let noble thoughts come to us from all and every direction in the universe". Here open mindedness is referring to only noble thoughts. In other words, one must necessarily have the anti-virus/ firewall, to filter and receive thoughts or ideas that are good or beneficially inspiring or useful. Noble thoughts inspire us to lead a peaceful life, and they aid growth of mind, eventually everlasting joy and peacefulness. Buddha says "We are shaped by our thoughts; we become what we think. When the mind is pure, joy follows like a shadow that never leaves."

Positive & Negative Thoughts

When we make notes of the thoughts and ideas that flash through our consciousness, we might be able to fill the pages of a book. The volume of the book would depend on the flood of these thoughts that happen to visit, linger, and have a free roaming luxury, inside of our minds. We might be surprised to find the content of the book to be worry, fear, remorse, grouses against everyone around us, including us. Who knows a few of those chapters might be filled with thoughts of happiness, gratitude, joy, and ecstasy et al.

In 2005, the "National Science Foundation" (independent federal agency of USA that supports fundamental research and education across all fields of science and engineering) put forth a summary that researched the thoughts of human beings on a daily basis. Approximately 12 thousand to 60 thousand thoughts per day per person, is what were, found to be present, through this finding. Guess how many were of the negative quality? 80 percent! Like a stuck record, these thoughts would keep playing in the mind over and repeatedly.

In a separate study "Leahy, 2005, Study of Cornell University, scientists "came to the realization of the fact: 85% of our worries do not see the light of the day. If at all 15% worries became a reality, 79% people who were in the study, were found to be better equipped to deal with their worry, far exceeding their expectation. However, dealing with the worry made them learn a worthwhile lesson. It is true that "97%"

worries in our mind are needless and almost always stem from being a pessimistic person. What is more, these so called "worries" made the mind to get very tired, and as a result, the body got tired too. Hamlet said that "there is nothing either good or bad but thinking makes it so."

According to Swami Vivekananda, "Mind is like a lake, and every thought is like a wave upon that lake. Just as in the lake waves rise, and then fall down and disappear, so these thought-waves are continually rising in the mind-stuff, and then disappearing, but they do not disappear forever. They become finer and finer, but they are all there, ready to start up at another time, when called upon to do so."

The Nun Study proved that a longer life can be achieved through positive thoughts. University of Kentucky conducted a study (1930), after studying the autobiographies written by nuns living a community life in their youth, in a convent. While being in the age group of 18 and 32 years, they were rated on a positivity scale; after 60 years, the surviving nuns, now between 75 and 90 years of age, were rated again. All of them scored very high for thoughts of positivity, and on life, irrespective on their circumstances.

The State of Our Mind' Quality Impacting Our Life' Quality

It is a common assumption that the state of our mind influences the reason for our actions, our lifestyle, and our achievement. Thinking can increase our heartbeat rate. Thinking can make our blood pressure rise or dip. Thinking can change the chemical composition of our blood. Thinking can make us happy and sad, be successful or a failure. In summary, the wellbeing of the state of our mind influences how well we live.

How can we alter what is in our mind? Can we monitor the speed of the waves of thoughts beating on the shore of our mind? Can we practice the presence of good thoughts, be able to appreciate the awesomeness of the current moment, do the action we are engaged in right now, in a superior manner, awaken creativity in our thoughts and actions, practice being grateful, make and keep connections, pay attention the things that matter to us? Let us conquer the negative thoughts in our mind, and stop them from exhausting us

To understand this, we must understand the concept of Conscious mind & Sub conscious mind. Mind can be divided into Conscious and Subconscious Minds. Majority of our emotions and behaviors have their roots in the subconscious portion of our mind. Conscious mind makes up our thought process and action in the woken state of mind. Being in the woken state, allows us to perform our regular activities of walk, converse, be engaged in work and so on. The subconscious mind is that part of our mind which remains in dormant state when we are getting the work done by the conscious mind. The subconscious works hand in hand with our conscious mind but we are not being to notice the activity being done by our subconscious mind.

OK - to make it simple, look at it this way: when we are learning how to drive a car, we are driving "consciously" - every action is a "conscious" action - like changing gears, applying brakes, turning and so on. After a few years of driving experience, we drive the car subconsciously. With practice, we can become very good at driving without being conscious of changing the gears and applying the brake, while being preoccupied with thoughts in our mind, and still drive well and have full control of the vehicle. This is achieved because we have learnt an activity and the repetition of that, becomes ingrained in our subconscious mind and gets imprinted in our memory. Our memory reserves are limitless, we can store and recall from here, always. Just as the saying goes, reap what you sow, our memory gives back to us, what we had committed to its care, as is.

Let us give an example of power of sub conscious mind with the real story of Arunima Sinha. Arunima Sinha, 24 years of age, a volleyball player of the national category, displayed exemplary mental strength

& firm conviction to etch her name in history going on to become the "First Female Amputee" to scale Mt. Everest & all the highest peaks in the seven continents". She met with a horrific incident when she was hauled out of a running train by some hoodlums when she resisted their chain snatching attempt. She sustained life threatening injuries & her left leg had to be amputated below the knee. She was shifted to AIIMS hospital for further treatment where she was provided with a prosthetic leg. Usually amputee patients take months, or even years, to get accustomed to their prosthetic limbs. She walked in two days. Loss of limb could have shattered her will. She mustered her courage & it was on hospital bed that she resolved to challenge her physical infirmities. She gathered her wits & nestled the dream in her sub conscious mind to climb the highest peaks from each continent around the world & hoist the Indian National Flag. This is a living example that the mind holds tremendous power over the body.

We have seen smokers, alcoholics, people with substance addiction, often try to break loose from these bad habits, but it is not that easy to rid themselves of the bad habits. Why? Because somehow, they have accepted in their thoughts and their subconscious mind that these activities give pleasure to them.

Repetition of any thoughts/determination/activities always train / teach our subconscious mind indirectly. Vice versa if they must leave these bad habits, they must send strong messages to subconscious mind through conscious mind regarding the bad impact of these bad habits. Repeatedly contemplating happiness in something divine, something noble, our mind will get attached there.

As per Neuroplasticity (a branch of neuroscience), every time we engage in physical or mental activities, neurons in the brain get fired. When these neurons are repeatedly fired in a particular manner, creating a neural path leading to that thought to repeat itself.

Just like we create physical habits with repeated actions, repetition of thoughts can be made into mental habits. It can be either detrimental or elevate us. For example, contemplate that anger is bad. We must never become angry; it will be harmful. If we contemplate again and again, we will find that our behavior will be transformed. Similarly, we can contemplate any wisdom and program our mind accordingly.

Reprogramming Our Sub-Conscious Mind

Believe it or not, if we have got command or we have practiced how to command or re-programme our subconscious mind we can drive our mind and body in any direction. There are three mind programming tools we can apply in our daily life. The first one is Power of Visualization and the second one is Power of Auto Suggestion and the third one is surround us with positive people.

Power of Visualization

A picture is worth a thousand words. A visual has the power to convey a thought or an idea faster and with better effect than words. A picture can convey much better. Our mind strength is only a small portion of the Universe's collective strength to create. We as well as the universe work in tandem, our mind is an extension of the universe mind. When we think a thought repeatedly, the power of the universe aids to bring it to fruition. When we want to attain something, picture it in your mind, repeatedly, with full conviction and having faith, we are helping our subconscious to convert them into real and true experiences Our mind does not make a distinction between the real life experience and one that is imagined. It will then begin to ready itself to adjust and absorb moments/chances to convert your mental images to see the light of day.

"Natan Sharansky, a computer specialist", was imprisoned for nine years in the former USSR, having allegations of working as a spy for the US. In the "solitary", he described the condition of the jail. He was in the Siberian jail for 400 days. His prison cell was 4 feet by 3 feet in size. In such condition, the body will deteriorate. He used to do antigravity exercises for his physical body. But what could he do for mental exercise? As a child he was fond of Chess. He designed a mental game of chess, and practiced his mental game played between himself and world champion chess player Garry Kasparov!

He stayed in jail for 12 years before getting released by Russia based on the request of American president Bill Clinton. He went to live in Israel and became a cabinet minister. In a demonstration match in Israel in 1996, Garry Kasparov was playing with 5 persons. But he lost to one person, namely Natan Sharansky. A reporter asked him how did he defeat the word champion? For 12 x 365 days he was defeating the world champion, every day in his mind. He had visualized again and again and programmed his subconscious mind for his victory against the world champion.

Power of Autosuggestion

Auto-suggestion is the easiest way to re-programme our subconscious mind. During waking hours, both our conscious as well as the subconscious are at loggerheads so to speak. At times, when we consciously want a state of mind, we find that the subconscious keeps a big grip on exactly the opposite.

In the process of moving from awake to sleep, our "brainwaves" hop from "Beta" to "Alpha" to "Theta", the destination being "Delta". During the "Theta" stage, it is believed that our mind is at its optimum state of openness to restructure our subconscious processes. Thomas Edison apparently said, "Never go to sleep without a request to your subconscious." In fact, each of us has used auto-suggestion at some point in our lives. The problem is most of us use autosuggestion to focus on negative things rather than positive ones. For e.g. we say, "I am tired", "I am useless", and then wonder why we feel that way. It has been said in ancient texts that, "The power of life and death lies in the tongue". This means, words are so powerful that they can either build or destroy you. So, we would rather use words to focus on positives instead of negatives.

Energy flows where attention does. If we think we are ugly, that is how we will be and if we think we are smart and confident, that is how we will appear, and our body language will show it.

The simplest way to harness the power of autosuggestion is positive affirmations.

Power of Positive Affirmations

These are powerful and positive sentences that we constantly repeat in our mind and heart till they get embedded in our subconscious mind. The power of autosuggestion is enormous, and it can be used in health, healing, prevention, relationships, or career in a huge way. Positive Affirmations have helped thousands of people make significant changes in their lives. It is encouraging to notice how widely this phenomenon is being spread and in a good way, the media has a big role to play in this. When an idea enters our mind, it analyses it and helps us to ready ourselves for the course of action we need to take. Repetition of "positive affirmations" make people sail through turbulent waters of difficult time, and land them safely on the safe shore. "I am building a powerful and profitable business." is a very good way of making positive affirmation to oneself. Scores of famous leaders and professionals in the business world, very actively use this process of positive affirmation mantra to reach their goal. E.g., If someone is a highly confused and not organized, the affirmation that is suitable to them could be "I am organized and in control." It is wise to profess our affirmations in the present tense, although it may or may not be so. When one is not wealthy, affirming: "I'm wealthy. I have plenty of money." This is helpful in taking us to a goal of attaining financial strength. It works very well when we discipline ourselves to follow a timetable: repetition of the affirmation 21 times, thrice daily, for example. Repeating affirmations, following it up with work in sync with our positive thoughts and experience the true strength of positive affirmations.

When we tell ourselves, "I'm going to have a great time on my date this weekend," our brain essentially absorbs the "good date" perception and sends off cupid arrows connecting the dots to ensure that your date is indeed going to be truly memorable. Speak positively to ourselves. Spoken words often in a repetitive manner influence the subconscious mind.

For example, Roger Bannister of England, was the first male to complete the mile-long run within 4 minutes. Till 1954, everyone that mattered were under the conviction that this was not possible to break the previously held record of 4 minutes. The thought was that the body was incapable of that speed and feared that collapse was inevitable. This was thought to be an impossible. He started to see it as possible. Bannister had finished in 3:59.4. He broke the world record. He did what was considered as "impossible". He made humanity proud, and with that created history. He paved the way for dreamers of achievement to be go getters. This became a reference point for everybody. In the same year 27 runners could do it. In next year, another 235 people did. When Bannister made it possible to cover a mile in less than 4 minutes, he challenged others to do it and prove a point: once you stop believing something is impossible, it becomes possible.

It made the world wonder, how after Bannister had broken the record, others could break through as well. The strength of the mind is what helped achieve this. The mind was given a suggestion that it is achievable, and the action followed, seeing success.

Surround Ourselves with Successful and Positive People

Thought is very infectious; may be even more than the Corona virus. A cheerful thought in you helps cheer others. A thought of anger produces a resentful mood in those who are in close proximity to the angry people. Keep a good, honest man and a thief together, there is a little possibility that he too might start to steal. A sober man in the company of a drunkard, might elicit a craving for alcohol in him. Being around positive people will elevate your mood and bolster your energy. When we are negative or feel depressed it might be due to our battle with our demons (thought process). Being around people with positive energy will help you make a change in your thought process quickly. Cultivate positive people in your life and try to interact with them; you will see a transformation in your energy level. Nearness to a sage helps create a unique calm; however being in the company of a bad and selfish person, we feel uneasy.

10

Power of Love

What is Love?

Right from an infant who has just entered into the world till the old man who is about to exit the world, love is the most sought after. Even the animals crave for love. Love is an act of giving, and it may be unconditional or conditional. It is very difficult to define love accurately. We often talk of parental love, brotherly love, family love, love for beauty, love for work, love for nature, love for animals and so forth. However, we can categorise all these love into four main types of love.

The first one is unconditional love. This love is also called divine love. We do not expect anything in return. We can also call this sacred love or selfless love. Best example is motherly love. Motherly love in that the relationship between mother and child is one of inequality; the mother has more responsibility to give love and care than the child. It is the toughest to cultivate this type of love.

The second one is Emotional love. This type of love makes us feel connected and bonded with a sense of liking someone by having similar thought process and finding things in common. Love grows deeper over time and connected so much that we use the word "soul mate". The best examples are love for siblings, children family and friends.

The third one is brotherly love. This forms the basis of every other type of love. Four components are contained within this – to care, to be responsible, to respect and to know, in our dealings with our fellowmen/ women. This love is what enables us to feel the oneness with humanity. The love between the mother and her child is different from love of a brother, (considering the entire humanity to be our family) A mother's love is unlimited, wherein she usually gives more to her children, and the children may or may not reciprocate in equal measure. Compared to this, love of a brother is for the entire humankind and generally given and received in equal measure, ideally.

The fourth one is Instinctive love. This is due to attraction by a combination of karma, pheromones, and subtle energy. Best examples are romance, physical desire, lust, or passion. This type of love may deceive us with effects of unwanted results or may lead to emotional love and develop into mature and stronger bond.

Love- Answer to the Problem of Human Existence

Love gives inspiration and an intense capacity to work. Both of which are essential for the progress of humanity. Love inspires people to discover, invent, serve people, behave morally, be a social change agent, be kind & compassionate, do charity work, share wealth, and grow spiritually. These are essential for the growth of mankind, and for a happy and peaceful world.

All the great personalities like Lord Buddha, Swami Vivekananda, and Lord Jesus have stressed on the power of love. Swami Vivekananda made the strongest observation about the power of unconditional love in these words. "Kindness and love can buy you the whole world; lectures and books and philosophy all stand lower than these". He further stressed how the world waits with open arms for pure, untainted love. It needs to be spread by all of us, with no expectation of reciprocity. Love knows no boundary. Love is blind. This means love makes no difference or discrimination. Love wins every time and does not get beaten. It has a unifying quality about it, drawing people together: Members of a family, community members, the citizens of a state and a country, and the entire world. Love is the main ingredient of universal wellbeing.

The Dalai Lama says "People were created to be loved, and things were created to be used. The reason why the world is in chaos is because things are being loved and people are being used."

Love is truth, Hatred is untruth. The absence of love disperses the humanity whereas love unites it. According to Buddha "Hatred does not cease by hatred, but only by love; this is the eternal rule" The only way one can get rid of hate in a person, is by offering the soothing balm that is love.

Jesus is the embodiment of love. Jesus says, "Love one another; as I have loved you." The Bible says: "There is no fear in love, but perfect love casts out fear. For fear has to do with punishment, and whoever fears has not been perfected in love."

Swami Vivekananda once said, "Jibe prem kore Jei Jon, shei Jon shebichhe Ishwar" This means one who loves a living being is serving God. God loves him who helps and loves humankind. Nature of nature is to love and help.

It is worth mentioning a famous quote of Mother Teresa "The greatest disease in the West today is not TB or leprosy; it is being unwanted, unloved, and uncared for. We can cure physical diseases with medicine, but the only cure for loneliness, despair, and hopelessness is love. There are many in the world who are dying for a piece of bread but there are many more dying for a little love". Pitrim A Sorokin, in his famous book "ways & power of love" says "Unselfish love has life giving force for physical, mental and moral health of people"

Love gives inspiration and an intense capacity to work. Both of which are essential for the progress of humanity. Love inspires people to discover, invent, serve people, behave morally, be a social change agent, be kind & compassionate, do charity work, share wealth, and grow spiritually. These are essential for the growth of mankind and a happy and peaceful world.

Love for Self & Others

Love for self- Nowadays, we often hear the term self-esteem, which is nothing but overall feeling we have about our own self-value. In other words, how much we appreciate and love ourselves. How much we feel we are worth. A person who has low self-esteem feels bad about himself/herself and has no confidence. Self-esteem can affect our mental health, how we behave, our decisions, our friendships, our success, and our life. We cannot truly love another until we know how to love ourselves. Self-love is nothing but the regard and value one has for oneself, about the principles and the ability to be distinctive. When we take good care of ourselves, our physical, mental, emotional wellbeing, we are said to practice self-love. It is very different from being selfish. One is not the other. Being selfish is when one thinks only of self, in total abandonment of concern for others.

Love for parents- If we talk of love of parents, it reminds us the story of Shravan Kumar shown in the "Ramayana". His parents were blind, as a result, carrying on the tasks of life was difficult for them. Shravan would help them with their work willingly and with a sense of pride. His parents had to just wish for something, it would be taken care of by their dutiful son. His aging parents had one wish, to visit four holy shrines of pilgrimage. Transportation was limited and unaffordable by them, keeping this in mind, the son devised something with so much love and devotion. He carried a basket each on either end of a long pole, on his shoulder, with their precious contents, his parents.

Recently, four brothers (modern day Shravan Kumar) from a Haryanvi village Palwal, took inspiration from Shravan Kumar's love and devotion, and helped fulfil their parents' desire for pilgrimage from Haridwar to Mansa Devi.

Love for god- Love of God is one of the most vital types of love. There is the element of religion in this and comes from the basic need a man must understand truth, meaning of life, and to bond with the eternal, the divine.

Love for Learning - This reminds me famous Mahabharata story of the student Eklavya and the teacher Dronacharya. The student Eklavya wanted to learn the use of the bow and arrow and become an expert. However due to various reasons, Dronacharya refused to mentor him. Eklavya returned home and made a resolve to learn archery, his devotion to the Guru prompted him to make a replica of Dhronacharya, out of mud. The statue of Drona constantly reminded him of the heights he wished to achieve and that propelled him to work hard. Eklavya reached the pinnacle surpassing Arjuna, Dronacharya's beloved student whom he had promised to make the best in the world. Arjuna had the luxury of getting personal instructions from Dronacharya all the time while

Eklavya only had the inspiration and determination with him. With just these two traits, he was able to surpass Arjun. Eklavya was interested in archery for the love of archery not for fame or his ego.

Love for the Environment- This reminds us the Khejarli Massacre in Rajasthan where community volunteers breathed their last breath, to protect those trees that they loved and kept sacred.

Love for animals- When human beings display love towards animals and form a bond with them, become friends with them, it is referred to as love for animals. When they love animals, be they pets or any animals all over the earth, human beings also become true to them, respect them, keep them from harm. Not only man, but animal counterparts also possess feelings of love and of being loyal, and friendliness. Several organizations such as PETA (people for the ethical treatment of animals) and others, endorse and uphold the rights and the wellbeing of animals.

Love for Service- Love that prompts you to love and serve fellowmen by which it is essential to exhibit kind acts towards others daily. Helping to keep our surroundings clear of dirt and garbage, assisting someone across a busy road, showing the way to someone who is lost, teaching youngsters little moral lessons, keeping company of the aged, cheering up a saddened individual are various examples of love for service. Contributing to charity causes and helping with the upkeep of a religious place, are acts that stem from the love for service.

Love for Sharing of wealth- Let us understand the wealth pyramid of the world to understand the business case of sharing wealth. 1 % of people in the world are controlling 70–80 % of resources. 90 % of population is working for 1 % of population. The annual Oxfam survey, 2019, which was keenly watched and discussed in detail at the World Economic Forum Annual had showed that globes richest 1% held a huge 50 % of the world's total wealth. The number of billionaires in the world is also on the rise. Wealth gap continues to grow, according to Oxfam report.

However, once love starts operating, everyone starts the sharing of wealth. Philosopher and poet Ralph Waldo Emerson said, "Without a rich heart wealth is an ugly beggar".

Time has come to discover ways and means of promoting selfless love and instilling a sense of cooperation and good will among people. This will inspire them to live a life of happiness for himself/herself and to others around him/her. This will also bring peace and harmony in the family, community, state, national & global level. People believe that it is easy to love. Though everyone has the same capacity to love, there are only a few who have really cultivated the art of loving.

Inculcating Love Through Spiritual Education

Three truths drive the loving heart: "discipline", "concentration" and "patience". This may be possible though spiritual education. Our essential nature is pure love and pure happiness. We can inspire love in our life by taking a few small and intended steps like doing meditations, practicing gratitude, and embracing forgiveness. To instil the strong spirit of love, we may give exposure to our people right from their childhood.

Further, it is also felt that even if a portion of the total global expenditure on military arms & ammunitions is spent on promotion of such selfless love, the word will be greatly benefitted. This is because, the total global defence budget increased to "$1822 billion" in 2018, an increment of "2.6" % from the previous year, as per the data from "Stockholm International Peace Research Institute" (SIPRI). The major players were USA, China, Kingdom of Saudi Arabia, India, and France whose collective budget made up for 60% of the worlds defence expenditure. Six Middle Eastern countries are among the total of top ten, being the top spenders: KSA (8.8 %), Oman (8.2%), Kuwait (5.1%), Lebanon (5%), Jordan (4.7%), and Israel (4.3%) of their respective GDP.

11

Power of Prayer

Transformation of One's Consciousness

We see scores of religious and spiritual literatures flooding the market from publishers, year in and out, and most of these focus on the power of prayer. All these books state that one of the greatest spiritual weapons is prayer. The power of prayer should not be underestimated.

Prarthana is the Sanskrit word for prayer, coined by two words 'pra' = 'intensely', 'artha'= 'to plead'. Prayer is discipline that is being practiced throughout all centuries in all parts of the world. Prayer is nothing but thanksgiving, giving in to a power that is much bigger greater than us. It is like renewing of the faith that we have in a supreme being, leading us to that enlightenment. Authentic prayer is a deep connection with the Divine present in everything and everywhere. Prayer brings about transformation of one's consciousness.

There are three tiers of reaching the state of spiritual fulfilment: through Gyan, pursuit of knowledge; Karma, acting upon that knowledge; and Bhakti, the means of attaining fulfilment through being devoted. The essentials to reach the goal are detachment from 'ego', putting an end to 'pride' and 'arrogance' in the search for God. Prayer is the journey to arrive at this destination.

Bhagavad-Gita says: "The virtuous ones who worship Me are four kinds, the man in distress, the seeker for knowledge, the seeker of wealth and the man of wisdom. Of these, the wise one, who is ever in constant union with the Divine, whose devotion is single-minded, is the best. For I am supremely dear to him and he is dear to Me"

When Do We Pray?

When do we pray? Do we pray to "cope with adversity? Do we pray when we are happy & prosperous? Or do we pray irrespective of our situation? But people rather than regular prayers, use prayer as their insurance policy, i.e., when in problem use it and when not answered condemn it.

Bible says, 'Pray without ceasing,' meaning always pray, daily, not as-and-when-it-pleases-me, and certainly not just when one is in trouble. 'The effective, fervent prayer of a righteous man avails much.' (James 5:16)

To quote the late Dr. Billy Graham, an American evangelist, "We are to pray in times of adversity, lest we become faithless and unbelieving. We are to pray in times of prosperity, lest we become boastful and proud. We are to pray in times of danger, lest we become fearful and doubting. We are to pray in times of security, lest we become self-sufficient."

Interestingly, as per the report titled "In Crisis, We Pray: Religiosity and the COVID-19 Pandemic" published by an economist at the University of Copenhagen, there has been sudden and dramatic increasing in the number of people googling the word "prayer". The data analysis has been done through searches spanning '75' countries. People looked for "Prayer" and this trend "skyrocketed during the month of March 2020," around the time when the current pandemic started spreading exponentially across the world. As per the report, there was a ratio between declared positive count (approximately 80000) and the strength of the prayers, that had been doubled. It is estimated that as more people get infected, and life of loved ones is lost, there will be a heightened fervour of prayer.

According to Mahatma Gandhi- "The purpose in prayer is to awaken the divinity in the depth of our heart. Man's need for prayer is as greater as his need for bread. As food was necessary for the body, prayer is necessary for the soul. True prayers never go unanswered. When the mind is full of prayerful thoughts, everything in the world seems good "

Offering prayer as a means of self-purification has been in practice in India since time immemorial. For example- the universal prayer Om Sarve Bhavantu Sukhinah..." (Let the People of the world be happy...) is used in the context of public prayers or mass chanting of mantras for a social cause.

"Om Sarve Bhavantu Sukhinah Sarve Santu Nir-Aamayaah | Sarve Bhadraanni Pashyantu Maa Kashcid-Duhkha-Bhaag-Bhavet | Om Shaantih Shaantih Shaantih ||"

Meaning: "May all become happy May none fall ill | May all see auspiciousness everywhere May none ever feel sorrow | Om Shaanti Shaanti Shaanti ||"

Another very popular prayer "Gayatrimantra" is from the Vedas. The prayer addresses the divine and the almighty. The prayer says "We meditate on that most adored Supreme Lord, the creator, whose effulgence (divine light) illumines all realms (physical, mental and spiritual). May this divine light illumine our intellect."

"Om Bhur Bhuvah Swah Tat-savitur Vareñyam Bhargo Devasya Dheemahi Dhiyo Yonah Prachodayat".

Prayer to Nature

Ancient philosophies around the globe classify the composition of the universe into 5 elements. The classification being earth, water, fire, air and space. One can have a firm hold on the knowledge of nature if we learn about these five elements with a deep sense of reverence.

In the Vedic literature, the five elements Agni or 'fire' (light and heat), Vayu or 'air' (energy and action), and Soma or 'water', have a divine nature, and help us to live life to the fullest. According to Vedas, three supreme deities of the Rig Veda, viz., Agni (fire), Vayu (wind) and Surya (sun) preside over earth, air, and sky, respectively. In Hinduism, followers worship the sun, as sun is the source of life, and it would become futile to go on without life. When you pray to Sun; you are not praying to a gaseous fireball but are praying to a symbol of a higher power which is sustaining life on earth. The Konark temple in Orissa, is dedicated to "Surya" (the sun) There are few more ancient Sun temples are in India, but Konark is still intact. The Konark Sun Temple has been elevated to the status of being a UNESCO World Heritage Site.

Interestingly, five aspects of prayer through purification breathing in relation with the five elements of nature are described by the Sufi teacher Hazrat Inayat Khan also. This prayer includes five breathing cycles focusing on each of the five classical elements.

Power of Prayer in Healing

Prayer has been associated with healing of diseases also. Dr Alexis Carrel, a 20th century Nobel laureate, for his work in vascular surgery, affirmed that {"Prayer is a force as real as terrestrial gravity. As a physician, I have seen men, after all other therapy had failed, lifted out of disease and melancholy by the serene effort of prayer. It is the only power in the world that seems to overcome the so-called "laws of nature"; the occasions on which prayer has dramatically done this have been termed "miracles." But a constant, quieter miracle takes place hourly in the hearts of men and women who have discovered that prayer supplies them with a steady flow of sustaining power in their daily lives"}

Various scientific studies have shown it is possible to be less anxious and be less depressed (or get over it completely) by the power of prayer. A reduced anxiety level in people to enable them to understand and take stock of the grim situation of COVID-19 with confidence and strength, all due to the power of prayer.

In order to further establish the theory that prayer can heal people, Dr. Dhanunjaya Lakkireddy, "cardiologist at the Kansas City Heart Rhythm Institute" has begun a study whether "remote intercessory prayer" helps in healing people affected by the virus. This will be observing a thousand patients in ICU, spread over 4 months of prayer study. There will be no change to the care procedure given to these patients, half the number of patients will be introduced to prayer, the other half will not be prayed over. None will have knowledge of the study. The prayers will be from five different religions, being Hinduism, Christianity, Islam, Judaism and Buddhism. Improvements in health will be measured on the five hundred patients, each one separately, the focus of observations being the wellbeing of their organs, ventilation need, and survival rate

It would have been a magnificent benefit to the humanity if the scientists directed their efforts to harness the infinite power of prayer though further research in spiritual science.

12

Sacred Music

Highest Form in Music is Spirituality

Music is a universal language, understood by all. As civilizations evolved, music too evolved as a part of the civilization's culture. Music is a medium used to call upon the almighty and to attain enlightenment. It is a very strong bond that connects us with our divine self, and to the all-pervasive universe. "Pandit Ravi Shankar", a renowned Indian Musician when questioned whether there was spirituality in music, answered: "The highest form in music is spirituality." The effect music has on our thought process, the emotions within, inner mind, and the wellbeing of our earthly form, is very great. Plato: "Music is a moral law. It gives soul to the universe, wings to the mind, flight to the imagination, and charm and gaiety to life and to everything." Music is another way to meditate. "Whoever can let himself dissolve into music has no need to seek anything else to dissolve into." – Osho

Songs & Music- Reawakening Moral Consciousness

Bhakti movement was an all-India movement of reawakening moral consciousness through devotional music. Bhakti Movement gained momentum from the 12th century and ended in the 17th century AD. "Jayadeva, Namdev Tulsidas, Surdas, Ravidas, Kabir and Mira" being a few of the most famous saint poets, in this movement. Interestingly, some of them belonged to economically lower strata of the society. Overcoming the stigma of "caste, colour, creed, they rose above it and spread the message of love and equality to humankind. They upheld qualities of love, compassion, justice and service in the form of songs and music. It also emphasised the strong bond between God and man, and the promise of attainment of eternal life by doing good and living a simple life.

Baul poetry, music and song are prevalent in Rural Bengal of India and Bangladesh. Their devotional songs and music are all about the connection between God and humanity, attainment of Godly freedom.

By incorporating love, consciousness in their poetry, belief in getting rid of social iniquities and injustice is reaffirmed. Baul Singers are the spiritual performers who sing the songs not just for monetary income or livelihood (or for becoming popular) but one of their primary missions is to sing songs to communicate spiritual messages to their next generations. The medium of the songs, the language is constantly evolving for relevance in our current world.

Like Bhakti movement of Hindu, Sufi traditions of Muslim community is well known for their music as a medium of spiritual expression. Sufi music is a form of religious expression influenced by the Sufi poets like "Rumi, Hafiz, Bulleh Shah, Amir Khusrow and Khwaja Ghulam". Qawwali is also a form of sufi music, along with many more practices that identify themselves with Sufism It is said that any person who has knowledge of both outer and inner life is a Sufi. Sufi poetry and music are nothing but expressing love and praising God, to reach the highest peak of enlightenment through the medium of the human voice. Interestingly, Sufi music are contemporary, and everyone seems to like listening to it. Hazrat Inayat Khan, the Founder of Sufism, in the west order in the west proponent of "Universal Sufiism" once said" "Music should be healing; music should uplift the soul; music should inspire. There is no better way of getting closer to God, of rising higher towards the spirit, of attaining spiritual perfection than music, if only it is rightly understood." All these movements preached the goodness of love, of compassion, of justice and selfless service through songs and music. What we need today is the practices of values and goodness. We need to learn from these movements and spread the moral and ethical values through spiritual music and songs.

13

Death is Inevitable

Countdown Starts from Day 1

The life span of a human being is very short, and this fact is realised when a person becomes physically weak. During youth, very few individuals realize the goal of life and the majority does not bother to understand that their days are numbered.

One should note that the countdown of any individual starts the on the day she/he is born. A person can amass wealth of millions, billions, and trillions but it is not possible for any person to live on earth even 40000 days. If we apply the logic that a person who maintains good health may live up to 80–85 years and very few cross 90 years, there are very few individuals who cross 100 years. Even if a person may live for 100 years, the life span is limited to 36500 days.

It is worth mentioning a few couplets (doha) of 15th century poet Kabir on "death". Kabir made it easy for us to understand it and to remove the mystery around it. His most popular Nirguni Bhajans, focus on death. The first of these Nirguni Bhajans {"Ud Jayega Hans Akela."} talks of how the swan, compared to the soul, will rise and elevate itself and disappear, and no one can try and stop it. Death comes stealthily, life evaporates from the physical body, and no one has control over this process. Several of Kabir's Dohas (couplets) discourse that our time on this earth is numbered. Kabir stresses the futility of doing unimportant things in life and how we should focus on self-improvement.

It is worth mentioning a quote from Vedic literature (Upanishad)-
"Live each day as if it were last, then you are able to choose wisely and
set your priorities admirably". In this it is imperative to mention one
of Kabir's greatest verses: "When you were born, you cried while others
laughed. Perform such deeds that when dying, you laugh while others cry."

Classic Buddhism Story on Death

When we discuss about dealth it is worth mentioning a popular tale in
Buddhism about Kisa Gotami, the life partner of a wealthy man. On the
death of an only child, Kisa Gotami sought others' help as she became
sorrowful, to the extent of almost losing her sanity. She was directed to
go to Buddha. The Buddha told her that only on the procurement of
"white mustard seeds" from the family where no death had occurred,
would enable him to bring back to life the dead child. Her search for
the mustard seeds from that ideal family of no death was totally futile.
The truth hit her hard, that no one is liberated from death. On her
return to Buddha, he gave her comfort and reiterated the truth that she
had confronted herself. She was awake in the real sense of the word and
eventually, she became an arhat (a perfected person who has achieved
spiritual enlightenment).

Do We Need to Fear of Our Own Death or the Death of Others?

Death is more of a universal fear. "fear of death," affects millions of
people worldwide. One of the positive ways to overcome fear of dealt is
to come to terms with the fact that death is imminent.

From the soul's perspective according to Bhagavat Gita, we all are
eternal souls, but we all have mistaken it as body. We go through so
many changes in our physical body as we developmentally progress
from infancy to old age. The body metamorphoses in unique ways
in a single life. Even the blooms and fruits in nature pass through

various transformation, of "birth, existence, growth, transformation, deterioration and finally death". In a similar way our physical body undergoes similar changes. The blooms and fruit on a tree are seasonal, while the parent, the tree continues to stay firm. However, the spirit soul does not undergo any changes. When the body metamorphoses in such a unique way in a single life, why do we fear losing the body upon death? With proper self-realisation, when we realise that we are souls then we don't need to fear of own death or the death of others.

Our body today is different from the one we possessed several years before today. Tremendous changes are taking place in the little particles that go into the construction of our body. The particles we possessed several years ago may not be present today. Cells in our body have an expiry date, and after that new ones are generated. The atoms inside the cell also change. We know that atoms go into the making of molecules, which make cells, tissues, and organs. In a study published in the Annual Report for Smithsonian Institution in 1953, most of the atoms got replaced every year, and it is cent percent replacement in a span of five years. We can stress that the atoms cannot be found if we look for them several years hence.

One of the positive ways to overcome fear of dealt is to be stoic and tell ourselves that death is inevitable. We are but cogs in a wheel, a small part of a larger design and find solace in the truth that everyone has to go through the same process. People are conceived, are born, and will die. Near-death researcher Norman Van Rooy once said, "Like the child being born, we have no choice but to yield ourselves to the unknown." We can admire our body and feel proud of our achievements in this life. The gift of life has been granted us for which we have to show gratitude and bow down when death comes knocking on our door.

We need to be in a state of readiness, be it in our thoughts or works, because death could come calling that very moment. Thomas Kempis (1380–1471) a Catholic monk and author of "The Imitation of Christ", advises that one should tell themselves that they may not last till the evening, and when the evening arrives, not to have the hope of seeing the coming day. That way one ought to be in constant readiness, and live that way, and one can be certain that death will never throw them off guard.

What Causes Death?

Let us examine the thought about the reason that causes death. The data available on the worldwide reasons that cause death, shows us that those causes undergo a lot of changes as people's lifestyle and healthcare facilities improve. These factors of life are directly proportional to the death rate in the world.

The main cause in 2017, was diseases of the cardiovascular diseases (CVD), and made up for 1/3 of the total demises. Cancers rank second around 17 percent. The leading global killer in 2017 were cardiovascular diseases (CVD). Cancers were the second largest, claiming around 17%. Respiratory diseases (including lower respiratory tract infection) claiming around 11.5 %. Overall, non-communicable diseases (NCDs) made up more than 73%) at global level.

The causes that were seen in the 20th century, varied from the ones we encounter today. From 1915 right up till 1945, mostly the most important reason that resulted in death for a population right from the very young to the middle aged, was preventive infectious diseases. Deadly diseases such as "Poliomyelitis (polio), diphtheria, tetanus, whooping cough, measles, mumps, and rubella" had been eradicated towards the end of the 20th century ever since early childhood immunisation was made mandatory, thanks to the progress of medical science. However, it may be noted that most of these NCD are due to air pollution, food, and lifestyle factors. Current lifestyle related health problems of obesity, diabetes, allergies, cancers, and neurological disorders are intrinsic to the design of a greed driven toxin-based agriculture and food system. We have conquered preventive disease but attracted lifestyle factor diseases. Interestingly, we are spending money on such toxic food to attract lifestyle diseases.

Part III

Cosmic Realization

"Every one of
us is, in the cosmic
perspective, precious.
If a human
disagrees with you,
let him live.
In a hundred billion
galaxies, you will
not find another."

Carl Sagan

14

Science and Spirituality

Science and Spirituality are not opposites but are complimentary

Let us understand if Spirituality has a connection with Science. What is the connection? Generally, we think that the two are poles apart. In truth Science and Spirituality are complimentary and are not at opposite poles.

Scientists across the globe are having consensus that the science includes orderly examination or enquiry of the world through observation and experimentation. Matter has always been in existence and man has been aware of it for time immemorial. People of science, nonetheless, will only accept it if they themselves have observed and tested them. Gravity has always been in existence, but it was Newton, who explained the law to the world in an understandable manner. Scientists, researchers, scholars and mathematicians like Newton, Galileo, Archimedes, Einstein and many more took it upon themselves and show in a clear way many of the facts and theories, so that everyone would understand them.

Human has physical form (the body), mind and intellect like the three receptors to perceive and experience. One experiences the world of objects through his/her physical body. One can experience the world of feelings through the mind. Similarly, one can comprehend his/her world of ideas through his/her intellect.

The truly amazing scientists have just tapped the spiritual power to achieve a balance among these three receptors – body, mind and intellect. They could notice and experience certain natural facts not easily observable by common individual and developed logical thoughts, standards and formulae. The scientists look at the outer world as their field of investigation. In other words, they investigate objectively (without any prejudice) the occurrences in the outer physical objective world. The spiritual way of observation takes into consideration the object, the subject, their ability to perceive, and the one who does the observation.

We need both science and spirituality, one without the other would not work. If both would work in harmony and in synchrony, that would be the best possible scenario. The realm of science and the spirituality world co-inspire even though they co-depend. As science needs spirituality, spirituality needs science. We need to unite science and spirituality. One without the other is not at all possible, as the realm of science would be devoid of the sense of right and wrong if spirituality was not a part of the process.

If people of science had no moral guidance, there would be a destructive force in play. Men and women of science would indiscriminately indulge in the creation and dispensation of weapons of mass destruction, would genetically modify against the natural scheme of things, create artificial intelligence with no soul, grow and rear animals in an inhuman way, and produce technologies that make waste, pollute and destroy mother nature.

Outer physical world is the scientists' domain of study whereas the inner expanse of experiences and the search for truth is the domain of the spirituality seekers. Science studies the earth or the world, on the other hand spirituality wants to understand man in his entirety and wholeness, good and bad included. Both these fields are interdependent and "inter-illuminating". Science needs to be guided by the gentle hand of spirituality and this would eliminate many problems our world faces in the current time. The realm of science must have meaning and be of value to humanity to help mankind.

Indian Ancient Wisdom on Astronomical Science

Curiosity to know the speed of light was an ancient urge. However, the quest for this knowledge started in 17th century. Physicist Galileo from Italy pioneered the measurement of the light's speed. Danish astronomer Ole Roemer put forth the fact that the speed of light travel is "finite". It was the American physicist Albert Michelson, in 1920, who finally came up with accurate formula to measure the speed of light, with the aid of a device that was octagonal and was a mirror that rotated. We now know that according to the worldwide standard, light travels in a vacuum and according to the current calculation is 186,282 miles per second.

It may sound strange, but the truth is that even before all these experiments and documentation, the sloka of Rigveda (composed several thousand years ago), stated that the light's speed to be around 185,016.169 miles per second. This is very close to modern value calculated with modern techniques. This shows the wisdom of Indian Rishis who were scientist as well. Many slokas of Vedas represent scientific theorems of modern days. Let us discuss one such theorem about speed of speed light and time.

[:Yojananam Dwe Dwe Shate Dwe Cha Yojane Aken Nimishardhena Krammana Namostute"

"Taranir   Vishvadarshato   Jyotishkrdasi   Surya   Vishvamaa Bhaasirochanam". (Rig-veda I,50–4).}

The meaning of the first verse is, Sun light speed is calculated using "Yojan & Nimesha", sunlight moves "2202 Yojans in Half Nimish". The second verse says "Oh Sun! (You) overwhelm all in speed, all visible, source of light. (You) shine over the Universe."} The two verses were elaborated in the 14th century by Sayanacharya, a minister in the court of the majestic Vijayanagar Empire of India. He says:

तथा च स्मर्यते योजनानां सहस्त्रं द्वे द्वे शते द्वे च
योजने एकेन निमिषार्धेन क्रममाण नमोऽस्तुते॥

(Tatha Ca Smaryate Yojananam. Sahasre Dve Sate Dve Ca Yojane
Ekena Nimishardhena Kramaman.)

{Sun (light) travels 2,202 yojanas in half a nimisha., In the Vedas, Yojana is a unit of distance and Nimisha is a unit of time. Distance covered =2202 Yojanas means 21,144.705 miles (Approx., 1 Yojana = 9 miles, 110 Yards). Time 1/2 nimesha = 0.114286 seconds (Approx.), hence, Speed of light= 185,016.169 miles / seconds.}

We cannot ignore just by escaping from the appreciation of ancient wisdom of Indian Munis and Rishis (spiritual scientists).

Albert Einstein and Spirituality

Let us also understand the view of famous scientist Albert Einstein in the context of spirituality. He said: "Everyone who is seriously involved in the pursuit of science becomes convinced that a spirit is manifest in the laws of the universe one in the face of which we, humans, with our modest powers must feel humble."

Spirit is like human breath or the wind in the environment. We are unable to see, touch or put a gauge to our breath, but have a sense of how it feels against our skin etc. In the same way one cannot see air and wind but can sense the effect caused by it. Wind creates movement among plants and trees, and the spirit affects human beings to move them. Human breath as well as the air around us is the lifegiving strength. What can be seen is held together by what cannot be seen.

Free Electricity with Cosmic Energy

To understand this, let us discuss the conversation between famous, influential spiritual leaders Swami Vivekananda and Nikola Tesla, the scientist in the domain of electricity. Nikola Tesla is not well remembered nowadays, but he was very famous in late 19ᵗʰ and early 20ᵗʰ century. He contended with Thomas Edison over the standardization of electric power transmission. Tesla backed Alternating current while Edison did Direct current. Tesla came on top with his AC mode of electricity transmission.

Nikola Tesla had met Swami Vivekananda in 1895. The meeting was arranged by French actress Sarah Bernhardt. To the surprise of both, the conversation in one evening meeting turned to topics of mutual interest. Among other things, Vivekananda and Tesla discussed the notions of prana (vital energy), akasha (ether), and kalpas (time), three elementary concepts of the Vedantic doctrine. Prana is understood as a unit of energy, akasha as matter, and kalpas as time. Nikola Tesla was highly impressed by the "Samkhya cosmology and theory of cycles" as per the Vedas. He was wonderstruck by the similarities of both the Samkhya theory of matter and energy and the modern physics.

Tesla was pleased to learn of Vedantic Prana, Akasha and the theories that can be adopted by modern science. According to Vivekananda, on that very night, Tesla assured him that such ideas could find an echo in modern Western science.

Swami Vivekananda later wrote in a letter in late Feb 1896 outlining the meeting, "Mr. Tesla thinks he can demonstrate mathematically that force and matter are reducible to potential energy. I am to go and see him next week, to get this new mathematical demonstration. I intend to write a book later in the form of questions and answers. The first chapter will be on cosmology, showing the harmony between Vedantic theories and modern science"

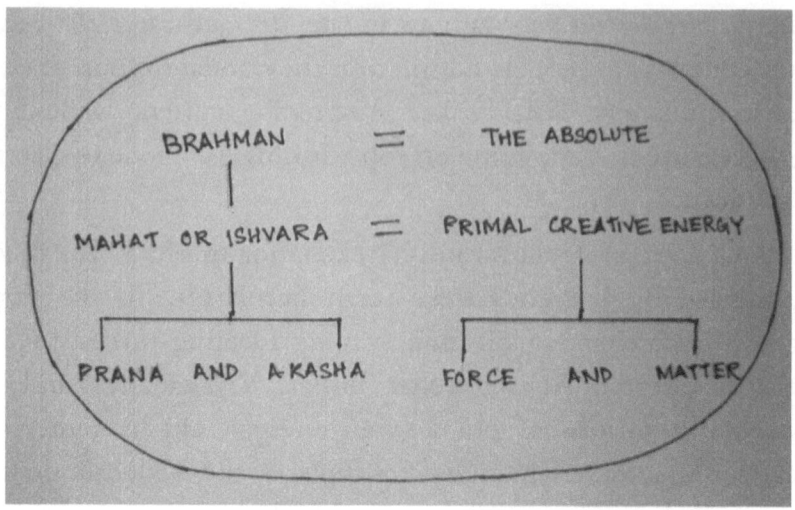

While working on Force and Matter, Nikola Tesla went in depth study of Prana and Akasha concepts, and this showed him a dimension to view the universe, that he was not aware of earlier.

He began seeing the world in terms of frequencies and energy that aided the study of his concepts on energy.

In an article, "Man's Greatest Achievement", published in 1907, Nikola Tesla made a mention of Prana and Akasa and he said "All perceptible matter comes from a primary substance or tenuity beyond conception, filling all the space. The Akasha or lumineferous ether, which is actually acted upon by the life-giving Prana or creative force as well, calling into the existence, in never ending cycles, all the things, and the phenomena".

Tesla, in his exploration of "Akasa" field, needed a process that was higher than the matter-converted-to-energy. His aim was to gather the original energy of the space, so the entire humankind could be its beneficiaries. He envisioned free energy to the whole world, via his "World Power System" (distribution of electrical energy with no wires being used, just the way broadcasting takes place). This vision did not see the light of the day, and the dream is very much palpable.

Spiritual Socialism

Without spirituality, it is not possible to appreciate the beauty of this creation and the greatness of human race. The nature which gives us everything needs to be understood in the first place. Such understanding will help us to truly respect the need for inculcating love and harmony among everyone.

If we see carefully, it is all about an individual development at micro level, then it is about a family, and a strong society comes into being, and it exists in its true form, and all these impacted into a formation of a great nation. Any narrow-minded approach in this chain of action would make the entire process and quality of any human and technological development as diluted as possible.

We need to support the weaker sections and at the same time need to promote potential ideas of positive change, we must create a place for our sustainable coexistence and this is nothing but the core of socialism, which is exactly achievable by keep spirituality at the helm of every action and intervention. Hence, this is the time for spiritual socialism to be put into action for a better world. Spirituality helps to create a moral society. It will inspire the entrepreneurs to innovate products/ services/ for the welfare of the society.

Spiritual knowledge forms the basis for our society. Social fairness and law and order become embedded in our communities, if everyone learns of spirituality of the various religions that are there. Money is yours but resources belong to society is the preamble of Socialism. And spirituality talks about sensible utilization of power in possession. Together it is time to realize the essence of spiritual Socialism for nature and humanity.

15

Cosmic Energy

Prana- Vast and Profound But Rarely Understood

"Prana", the force of life or the vitality that drives the living beings into activity. In Sanskrit, "Prana" is in two parts- 'pra' = 'to exist before': 'ana'= 'an atom'. So 'prana' is what has been there ahead of an atom. The ancient Vedas had knowledge of atoms a millennium prior to being discovered by scientists with the use of a microscope. Several cultures had the awareness of 'prana'. The Chinese call it 'chi' and 'qi'; In Japan, they refer to it as 'ki'; the Maoris call it 'mana' and the Greeks call it 'pneuma'. The Bible has a word for 'prana' and that is 'the holy spirit'. One feeling over the universe but many names given to it.

"Prana" is immeasurable, has no form and hence no taste. It is a feeling one has in the innermost of our physical body. We can call it as the connection between atoms and as the vital force. It is omnipresent. "Prana" filled things or beings are vitality filled. E.g., fruit freshly plucked from a tree, is filled to the brim with vitality. The same can be said about a group of people who are in harmony, without any skirmishes, are said to be full of 'prana'. Reference of 'low vibration' or 'high vibration' may be heard sometimes, while talking of a person, a group of people etc. which goes to demonstrate that 'prana' is the interaction between atoms.

People having a high level of 'prana' have a natural emission of love, cheerfulness, and harmony. Those people are said to have high vibrations and they tend to emit a good mood around them, because they have a radiance about them that is so visible and marked. The opposite can be said about people with a low 'prana'/vibration and they tend to evoke feelings of unease, disturbance, envy and even anger. To evoke these kinds of feelings, they do not even have to speak and do anything to cause it. Their mental makeup is such that it gets emitted around them. Low 'prana' people tend to drain other people of their vitality instead of helping boost it.

Even places can possess variation of vibrations, high or low. Some places with a high vibration, are good places to be in, while the reverse is true of places that are low vibrational. Forests, flower gardens, beaches, meditation spots, religious places have high vibrational quality which help you to lift your mood, feel inspired and be creative, or just experience enjoyment. Places that are "low vibrational" leave you feeling trapped, tired, or fearful, being in that vicinity. Ones prior experiences and connections can cause this to happen. Some examples can be a classroom, place of work and so on depending on the environment.

Food too tends to be vibrational. A "high-vibe" meal is fresh, well made, tasty nutritious and can boost your wellbeing and health. A high vibe meal is one which is fresh, comprised of plants of the earth and not been overly cooked. It is said that Food that is prepared by loving hands also raise energy vibrations to the food. It nourishes us spiritually. A "low-vibe" meal can be overcooked and listless. Refrigerator stored food, microwave cooked, deep fried food, sweet candies and aerated drinks can be referred to as low vibrational foods and they make you sluggish or feel heavy and energy-less."

We should appreciate the modern take on "Prana. "Prana", the vitality deep within us, around us as well is all encompassing. Our thought process makes up our actuality, our intent and our lifestyle affect our "Prana". All around us is energised, there is attraction between similar energies. The choice of a "high vibration" or a "low vibration" is in our thoughts, what we speak and foods we consume etc. People or places, can fill you with vitality or drain that vitality, depending on our life's choices concerning our physical, mental, and spiritual wellness that go to influence our "Prana".

"Prana" in the creation, be it the 'planet', an 'asteroid', a tiny blade of grass' or the mighty tree, is what goes to give it that elixir of life. Without prana, everything is formless, it would wither away and become extinct.

In the macrocosmic level, prana has a host of vitality. Each created being is afloat in a gigantic space of essential lifeforce. This form is referred to as 'cosmic prana'or "Mahaprana". It is in this state everyone imbibes their existence. The measure of 'prana'that gives life force to an individual is called individual prana. It is distinct from "Mahaprana" although the prana is essentially the same.

16

Sacred Tools of Well Being

Whole Person

To start with, let us understand the meaning of 'healthy person'. According to WHO, "Health is a state of complete physical, mental and social well-being and not merely the absence of diseases." Wholeness" has become a buzz word. Wholesome food, wholesome health. Now a days, we also hear the term "Whole person"- the wholeness in a person. The whole person refers to the person who is physically, emotionally, intellectually, and spiritually healthy. Only the whole person can build a new world, a new world order and a new humanity.

Energy Hubs and Channels

Inside of the human body there is an intricate and beautiful web of "Nadi"s (energy channels) that channelize this life force through the entire body. Prana uses this medium, via the channel of 'Nadis'. Yogic system has mapped 72,000 such energy channels. 3 major ones being:

Ida – found on the left of the spine, that makes up the introverted lunar channel. This is connected to the left nostril and gives a cooliing effect to the body.

Pingala – located to the right of the spine that makes the extroverted solar Channel. This is connected to the right nostril and gives a heating effect to the body.

Sushumna – Located along the center of the spine. This is the central passage, where the energy of "Kundalini" awakening flows through.

All the Nadis need to be working fully well without a blockage, for us to be in good health and have a happy disposition. Since almost all of us have some physical or emotional disturbance, which goes to prove that our "Nadis" do not function well and may need to be balanced.

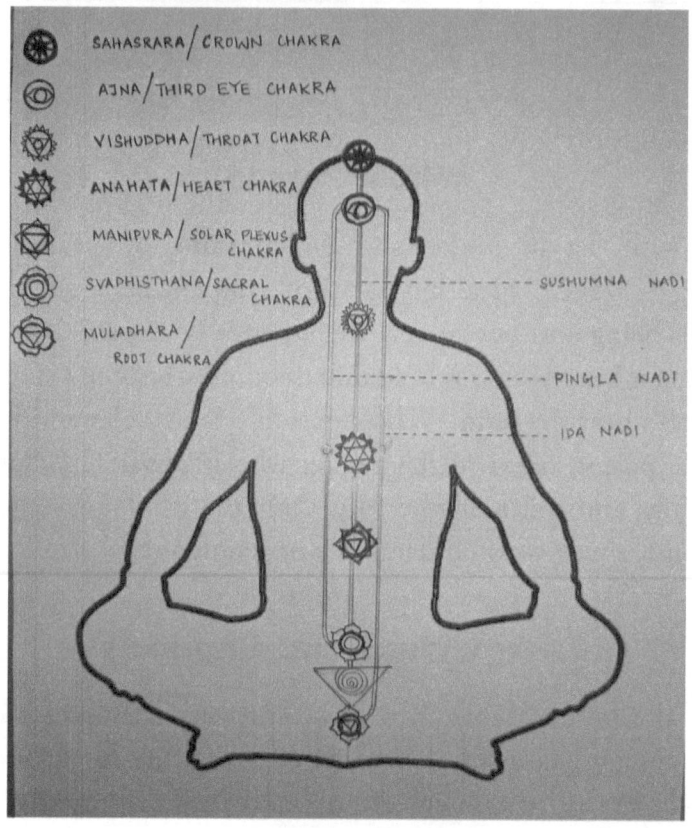

Nowadays there are lot of talks on "chakras". These are powerful energy centres. Just like Nadis (energy channels), chakras are of subtle nature and do not have any physical existence. The Nadis meet in a specific way to create an energy vortex (chakras). There are 7 key chakras. Essentially, chakras are energy hubs or centres. Chakras, the headquarters in your body, help to regulate smooth flowing of spiritual lifeforce from your Root Chakra right up to your Crown Chakra.

Purification of Energy Hubs

Free flowing "Prana" in our body and mind ensures that we feel healthy and energised. When this energy is blocked, tiredness and illness follow. It is possible that you have a chakra that is clogged or stuck. This can interfere with day-to-day life, but it can also create a spiritual block. This could start out as psychological symptoms: feeling distant, unable to concentrate, a lack of inspiration, also the onset of depression. Therefore, Chakra (the energy hubs) purification is vital to keep our spiritual energy free from negativity. How do we achieve this? Several practices exist to purify the chakras. These chakras can also be purified through yoga, meditation & conscious breathing (Pranayam) techniques.

Aura Vs Prana

Prana in the cosmic is Cosmic energy. This is the energy of the Consciousness. This is the vitality of awareness. This is the vitality that oversees the smooth running of the cosmos. It is all pervasive, in the constellations, the space around us, all over.

We always draw from this well of energy, however, our preoccupied mind, keeps us from getting the optimum benefit out of it. Science proves that within the human body, levels of life force vibrating at a given rate. This vibrating life force gives rise to a magnetic field on all sides of our body. Human bodily processes of breathing, assimilating the food, the thought process and blood circulation make up several electro-chemical reactions. This magnetic field and electrical energy fields interact to form "The Bio-Energetic Field". This field is called 'Aura' and its influence extends up to four to five feet from our body. Just like human beings, plants and animals, including inanimate objects have 'aura.' Aura consists of primary colours, as in the rainbow.

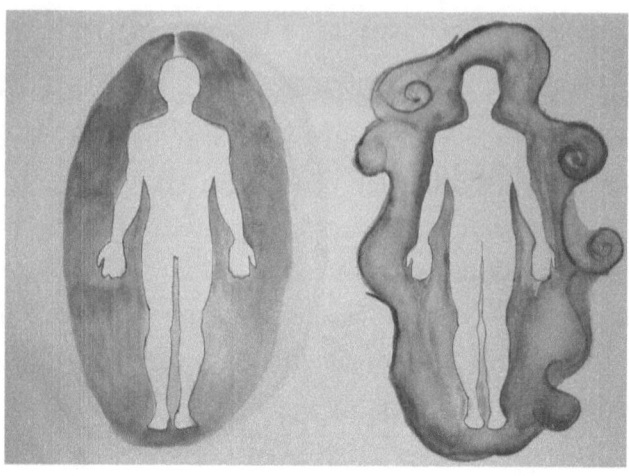

The physical and the emotional wellbeing of a person can influence the colour and the size of their aura. Happy people with a positive disposition have a wide, uniform and bright aura, and those sad, negative people have a tiny, dull, irregular shaped or dark aura. Any imbalance caused to the normal running of the chakras, caused probably from impaired wellbeing, affect our aura. In medicine, this comes across as diseases or illness, namely cancers, diabetes, and hypertension. It could also result in imbalance of the mind or our psychological wellbeing, and cause depression, insomnia, bipolar trends and so on. Hence even before the disease becomes manifested in the form of symptoms, the aura can be purified and brightened up.

But can the aura be seen? Yes, it can be seen through Kirlian photography. To an ordinary human being, Aura may be seen a pattern or radiance around a person or object. Aura has a distinct form comprising of the VIBGYOR colours. These colours have specific meanings. Aura photography was discovered by the Russian scientist Semyon Kirlian in 1939. The name aura photography and Kirlian photography are both used widely. In 1961, Kirlian and his wife published their first article about electromagnetic field that surrounds the human body in the Russian Journal of Scientific and Applied Photograph. Energy field Images captured through Kirlian photography have been very popular in energy treatment (a field of alternative medicines). Several advancements have come about, that use improved technology and cameras to give ultra-modern results.

How to Receive Cosmic Energy

It is worthwhile to mention here that Paramhansa Yogananda in his Book "Autobiography of a Yogi" has given detailed account of a lady named Giri Bala in Bankura district of West Bengal who has gone without food and drink for over half a century (picture of that lady with Yogananda).

Upon rigorous investigation of her non-eating state by maharaja of Burdwan, it was found that she used to adopt specific yoga technique to energise her body with cosmic energy from the ether, sun, and air.

There is abundant cosmic energy in the cosmos. Abundant energy is available in hill tops, forests, the natural environment, and pyramid shaped houses. What we need today in the society is people with holistic health. To have better emotional and physical health of an individual, we need to leverage cosmic energy. There is abundant cosmic energy in the cosmos. Cosmic energy cleanses all etheric areas because of its heavy flow. When these etheric patches are cleansed, we get freed from all our illness.

We can brighten our aura by increasing our bio-energetic field though cosmic energy. This cosmic energy is free of cost. There are various natural methods at zero cost, to imbibe cosmic energy. This energy can be channelized by controlled breathing exercises or energy healing techniques. However, the best and simplest ways to acquire this cosmic energy is through 4 key approaches.

The first one is meditation. This is the best and preferred method of restoring our mind's calm state. With the mind in a calm condition, with no preoccupations, that, we open ourselves to an abundance of cosmic energy. With meditation, our mind reaches focused state and are ready for the shower of cosmic energy blessing. In energy terms, one hour of meditation is equivalent to six hours of sleep. Our mentor says that when we do meditation in a group, we can receive three times the energy. We will discuss further, on meditation, later in this chapter.

The second approach is outer purification. Just as the purification of our thoughts of negativity, it is equally essential to have clean surroundings. If we follow a simple method of 'Buy one, give one', i.e., with the purchase of a new item, we must practice giving away something we had had, to a needy individual, to create the space for the new purchase. One might also practice 'when in doubt, throw it out'. If we have not used an item and are unsure if we ever might use it in the future, give it away to clear the space taken up by it.

The third one is Present moment awareness. It is the key to mindfulness. It refers to monitoring the current moment and not dwelling in the past or imagining the future. Dwelling in the past and worrying about the future generates toxins in the body. To harmonize emotions, there is a need to use breathing techniques.

The fourth approach is limiting our ego self-talks. It is common to indulge in egoistic utterances. A simple test to detect this is to pay attention to the number of times we use "I" in our utterances. A survey that was done discovered "I" to be the most frequently used word in the English language. With mindfulness and a little care, we can avoid using words manifesting ego. This is one step closer to receiving cosmic energy.

Yoga- Best Technology in the World

We have been practicing yoga for more than 15 years. As a part of our spiritual enhancement, we have learnt to give importance to "asanas" (yoga postures), "pranayama" (breathing exercises) and meditation (resting the mind and attaining a state of consciousness or to stabilise awareness). These three activities are among 8 branches of Yoga.

Let us understand the meaning of Yoga and origin. The first use of the word 'yoga' comes from the Rig Veda, which dates to 1700–1100 BCE, or about 3000 years old. Generally, we understand that yoga means twisting our body bending our limbs to remain physically fit.

Yoga is not only about only physical well-being and fitness but much more than that. Yoga means union. "Yoga" was derived from the Sanskrit root yuj meaning 'to unite'. A question may arise - Union of what? Union of three dimensions of life - body, mind (thoughts and emotions) and energy. Therefore, the primary purpose of yoga is to integrate all these three dimensions of life. It is the science of aligning these three dimensions of life. When these dimensions of life are in perfect harmony, the best of our ability will flow out of us. We can say that it is a practical technology to awaken human potential or human possibilities.

The Yoga Sutras of Patanjali compiled sometime between 200 BCE and 500 BCE by the sage Patanjali in India talks about Aṣṭanga yoga. In this book, we will talk about the eight branches of Yoga called eight-fold paths or eight limbs (Aṣṭanga- Ashta=eight, Anga=limb).

The first branch of yoga called "Yama"- dealing with the moral aspects in a person, directing him to behave with principles in his life. The five "yama" are "Ahimsa" = non-violence; "Satya" = truth; "Asteya"

= no stealing; "Brahmacharya" = life of celibacy; "Aparigraha" = state of non-possessiveness.

The second one is called Niyama which deals with self-discipline and spiritual observances. The five "Niyamas" are "Saucha": cleanliness/ freshness or purity; "Samtosa": contentment; "Tapas": heat/ascetic practice; Svadhyaya: Learning the sacred scriptures and of one's deep self; "Isvara pranidhana": surrender to God. The third one is "Asana" (body postures) used in yoga. By using asanas, we become disciplined, can concentrate, both being very essential to meditate. The fourth is "Pranayama". Controlling our breath, used to become highly conscious of our respiration, at the same time keeping a connection alive among the breath, mind, and our emotions. We will further discuss Pranayama later in this chapter. The fifth being "Pratyahara", meaning detaching our senses from the environment around us, and be in a receptive state to listen to our inner voice. During this stage, one withdraws attention of the outer world and its distractions. The sixth being "Dharana" (Concentration). While concentrating, we put our thoughts on a slow mode, to enable concentration on a single aspect of the mind. We use this process to get better at attention and intention. The seventh one is Dhyana or Meditation, the stage where the mind has been quieted, and in the calmness where there are ideally no thoughts at all. We shall discuss this in later part of this chapter. The eighth one and the final stage is "Samadhi". At this stage we attain an intense oneness with God, a pure connection with all the living and experience ecstasy

We believe that this knowledge of yoga has universal values. In other words, it is valuable for every person in this world just like law of gravity or law of relativity. The knowledge and wisdom of yoga is being embraced across the world.

Yoga is a wholesome way of taking health in our hands and of experiencing wellness. All over the world, Yoga is popular and is practiced in variations of techniques. The numbers following Yoga today is seeing an exponential growth. Due to Yoga's worldwide popularity,

UN, decided that 21 of June would be marked as the "International Day of Yoga". This is helping in a big way, to increase awareness of Yoga and its beneficial effects on the humanity.

Breathing is Everything

There are four different sources of energy we get to survive. The first is food, the second is sound and adequate sleep, the third is a meditative state of mind and the fourth one is the breath.

Breath is the most important. It is the breath which we have ignored or forgotten. 90 % of the impurities in the system are thrown out of the body through the breath. Every time we exhale, we get rid of carbon dioxide. Toxins are getting ejected and the blood gets purified.

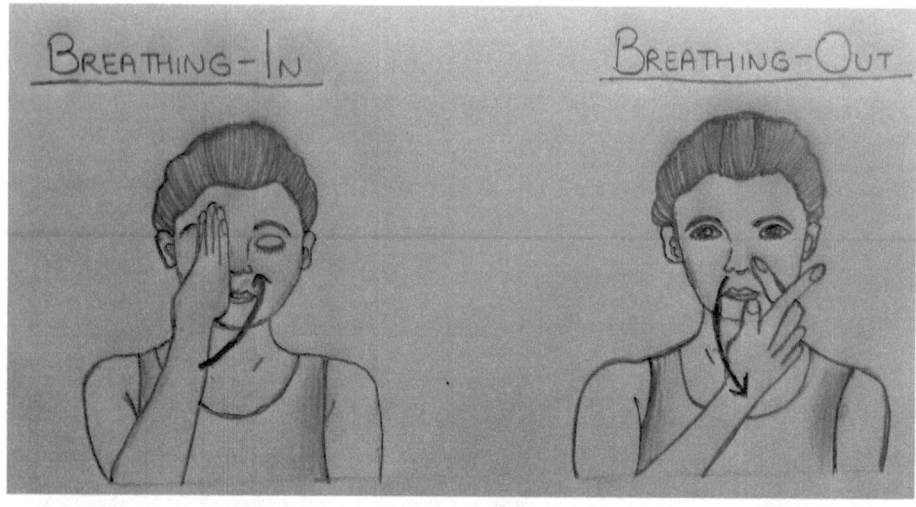

Breathing pattern is different for one who is depressed, unhappy, anxious, and tense because breath is a link between body and mind and for every emotion, there is a corresponding rhythm in the breath. Therefore, our breathing method has an important effect on our health and wellness; the stress we endure that at times make changes in our physical entity, like raising or lowering of our blood pressure.

To breathe, is the most tangible representation of the vital energy - prana. In other words, Breathing is believed to be the life force that connects you to the entire universe. Human breathing is controlled by your autonomous nervous system, which means that most of the time you breathe unconsciously, and do not regulate the quality or speed of your breaths. The 15th century yoga manual "Hatha Yoga Pradipika", says one needs to regulate breath to be able to enjoy good health, long life, and contentment. The yogic method of being aware of breathing is nothing but "Pranayama" (Sanskrit word for "extension of the life-force") and has been in practice for thousands of years and goes to heal the mind and the body.

Nowadays, conscious, or controlled breathing technique has become a regular therapeutic tool used globally in positive psychotherapy, positive psychology, stress management and many other fields. There are only two ways of breathing: conscious and unconscious. In the past few decades, western scientists have been exploring how the nervous system can be affected with controlled, conscious breathing. For example, by regulating the quality of breaths—length, rhythm, intensity - you can switch from the sympathetic to the parasympathetic nervous system, and vice versa.

Research studies show how we can have a control over our heart rate, regulate skin temperature and the functions of the digestive system by focusing on our breathing. This knowledge was in the treasure trove of "Yogis" for thousands of years. How many times have we heard the term, "Take a deep breath" being uttered, in conversations, in therapy/training sessions? According to Dr David Anderson of the National Institutes of Health (medical research centre of Government of USA), the practice of minutes-long deep breathing every day, can help regulate irregular blood pressure. He proves how the quality of our breath has a consequence over regulation of blood pressure level. It is research that shows a correlation between practiced controlled breathing and the size of the brain, enhancing cortical thickness.

There are two key conscious breathing techniques. The first one is "Anapanasati" (Basics). It is believed that the "Anapanasati" technique was created by the Buddha himself. The initial practice is simple, and its purpose is for you to feel the sensations caused by the movements of your breath in your body. The second breathing technique is "Pranayama". Several pranayama breathing techniques exist, namely "Bhastrika" (Bellows of breath), "Kapalabhati" (shining breath), "Dirgha" (complete breath), "Ujjayi" (success breath), "Nadi shodhanam" and many others which are not being explained here. These simple techniques can be learnt and practiced under the strict guidance of competent teachers

Meditation- Day to Day Life and Management

Have you ever experienced slightly embarrassment when you failed to recall the name of an acquaintance whom you met after a long gap? For that matter, do you rack your brain to recall the name of a movie or the name of who acted in it? To forget is very common, but to forget when one is still young is a little unusual. The span of our attention span refers to the length of time one can concentrate on something: a thought, job or talking, without swaying and losing focus. Too many messages, too many options and too little time to deal with them. Attention span of human beings has dipped to 12 seconds in 2000, and further down to 8 seconds and we can attribute this the mobile phone bombardment. Even Goldfish can hold a thought for longer. It can focus on a task or object for 9 seconds. We are worse than the goldfish.

Nobel laureate Herbert A. Simon observed, "a wealth of information creates a poverty of attention" A study, that researchers at the "Technical University of Denmark" says that the total global attention span is diminishing because of the volume of information offered to the public. Researchers are alarmed that the explosion of technology and social networking is helping decrease people's ability to focus. Think about how much stimulation we ourselves are exposed to daily. Basically, the brain is on constant overdrive.

Scientific study with experiment, shows that people can better focus on tasks at hand, for longer periods, if they meditate. This will help calm them and improve their ability to deal with anxiety, depression, and post-traumatic stress disorder. Through meditation the entire self is recharged and vitality returns; sharpens the mind its capacity to indulge in intellectual pursuits. It is not a novel concept that meditation does have beneficial effect. Effort is being made by scientists to figure out what is the relationship between meditation and the improvement of the physical and mental health and how it can do so reliably.

Meditation culture is required at all three levels- community, business, and government level. Let me start with business. Meditation has made deep inroads into the corporate world. Nowadays, big Businesses are promoting meditation practices in the workplace. This is to increase creativity, innovation, and productivity of the employees.

In the recent few years, a lot of big companies viz, "Google", "Yahoo", "Nike", "HBO" and many more have incorporated meditation spaces in their facility. Their employees can use these spaces, some companies even offer free meditation sessions, group meditation workshops and classes. "Salesforce" provides a room per floor dedicated to meditation. "Apple" gives a half-hour meditation break daily; not to mention the fact that all their offices all over the world have a dedicated meditation room. "Studies show meditation improves your creative and critical thinking, reduces stress, and smoothed out interpersonal relationship".

At the government level, the Government of India, multiple State Governments, and many PSUs across India have introduced meditation training course for the government officials with an objective of increasing worker efficiency, bringing integrity, ethics and citizen service centric mentality in the government. For example- Maharashtra Government has passed a resolution that will allow government workers to take leave to participate in a 10-day Vipassana meditation course. Railway Board of Government of India has a policy in place that states the participation of Indian Railways personnel in Meditation/Yoga/

Spiritual and other related programmes. At least 185 MPs in UK have taken mindfulness courses provided at the Houses of Parliament and mindfulness-based cognitive therapy courses are prescribed by the NHS. It is good to introduce such inner transformation exercise for the elected representatives and the public servants.

Meditation has been introduced in many jails of India. Two well-known filmmakers Ayelet Menahemi and Eilona Ariel from Israel were given access to maximum-security zones in one of the world's largest prisons Tihar Jail in New Delhi. Their documentary film, 'Doing Time, Doing Vipassana' is an eloquent story of how deeply Vipassana meditation had been beneficial to even the most condemned of human beings - murderers, terrorists, rapists and ruthless gangsters.

Similarly, at community level, it would be appropriate to introduce such inner transformation exercises right from students in every educational institute. A recent meta-review of on the influence of meditation in schools, corroborated the results from 15 studies involving 1800 students from Australia, Canada, India, the UK, the US and Taiwan. It proved that meditation mostly favoured the change that brought about 3 significant outcomes for students: "higher well-being, better social skills and greater academic skills". Myriad academic and learning skills impacted quicker assimilation of information, improved focus, concentration, memory resulting in higher creativity and thinking flexibility.

In today's stress and tension filled world, people are practicing meditation and enjoying peace. As per the recent Google data, the number of searches on yoga and meditation apps, like 'yoga for beginners' and 'mindfulness' went up by 65% YoY. "52 million" users facilitated the download of the top 10 meditation apps in 2019. Launch of over 2,500 meditation mobile applications took place after 2015. Some popular inner transformation techniques being used now-a-days are: Vipasaana meditation, Kriya Yoga, Hatha Yoga, Transcendental Meditation, Pranayama, Sudarsan Kriya, Raja Yoga, Siddha Samadhi Yoga (SSY), Sahaja Yoga, Pyramid Meditation.

A mention of the Pyramid Meditation is required here. Pyramids the size of their home/office, for the purpose of meditation are being built by people.

The theory that an apple kept under a pyramid will not rot for 10 days, has been proven. Used razors and knives stay sharpened. Several reports of the repeated use of a blade for more than a year, when stored under a small pyramid, have come to light. By meditating under a pyramid, the energy centers get activated easily. The pyramids have three times better energy field. Pyramid meditation and the use of pyramid power is gaining popularity. When we talk about pyramid meditation, we cannot ignore the work of "The Pyramid Spiritual Society (PSS) Movement". This movement comprises involvement of more than a couple of thousands of independent and autonomous pyramid spiritual societies and spreading awareness to millions of people across all states in India and twenty other countries.

Amid the lockdown due to Corona virus pandemic, we can see everywhere around the world, people have become much more mindful about their health. Such crisis requires us to remain calm, and resilient. With social distancing being recommended by governments and many people self-isolating, we may find our mental health taking a toll, because not being able to go out or social interaction can lead to stress and anxiety. This is the time to embrace spirituality. While it is quite important to stay calm and relaxed in these testing times, the better way is to do it through meditation. Harvard Medical School in their latest health guideline have declared that yoga, meditation, and controlled breathing are "some tried and true ways to relax".

Power of Nature in Healing

Technology and industry have widened the gap between us and nature. Our dependence on nature continues. It is a universal truth that being in nature is beneficial to us. We do not need researchers to awaken us by telling us that human beings living close to nature, enjoy superior physical as well as mental health.

Forest walks and spending time in it known as shinrin-yoku or forest bathing, is widespread in Japan which can also be preventive health care. A study conducted in Tokyo, Japan shows that almost all people showed higher natural killer cell activity and anti-cancer proteins in the body after the forest trip (about 50 percent increased) for 2 days & 3 nights.

Another study conducted by a forest-therapy expert and researcher at Chiba University in Japan, discovered that people who had spent time walking in a cedar forest had lower levels of the stress hormone cortisol, that caused blood pressure and the immune-system irregularities. In the US too, they proved that patients who had a window view of cedar trees healed from surgery much faster than those who viewed a brick wall.

In the context of power of nature in healing, it is worth to mention the concept of grounding or earthing. We have failed to have that connection with the earth because we no more tread bare footed, but wear shoes with synthetic soles that act as a barrier between us and the mother earth.

Research has shown barefoot contact with the earth can produce nearly immediate improvement in the body, which aids better sleep, pain reduction and reduced muscle tension and decreases stress. This is because earth's surface contains negative charge and helps to produce electrons that could neutralize free radicals there by becoming antioxidants. We may think that antioxidant can come only from food. But this is not so. It can come from earth also. We need to be grounded. The question may arise how do make grounding. It is good for us to walk barefoot on grass, moist soil, sand, gravel, or concrete, not synthetic surfaces.

We need to strive for more greenery and more grounding to have healthier and longer lives?

17

Doctrine of Ahimsa

Ancient Wisdom- Nonviolence

Nonviolence is nothing but the exercise of not harming oneself and others, be it humans, plants, animals, or environment. It goes against the natural order of things in the universe and non-violence is necessary to live in harmony in this universe. The Upanishad had the earliest evidence of the word "Ahimsa". It forbids violence against all living beings ("Sarvabhuta"). Someone who truly practices Ahimsa, is saved from the cycle of rebirths. Living beings have a bit of the almighty and harming another being is a sin against God and self, giving rise to apt repercussions.

Nonviolence or Ahimsa is an essential virtue and tenet of Jainism, Hinduism, and Buddhism. In Buddhist texts Ahimsa (is part of the Five Precepts, the first of which has been to abstain from killing. In Jainism, the understanding and implementation of Ahimsa is very strict, much more so than in any other religion. Killing any living being out of passion is considered "Hiṃsa" (to injure) and abstaining from such an act is "Ahimsa". The vow of ahimsa is the most important of the 'five vows of Jainism'.

Ahimsa should begin at the basic level of the individual, of the family, and of the local community across the globe. We should all strive for a community of peace and harmony. Ahimsa recognizes the necessity of protecting the earth's animals, the young children as well as the unborn. All the innocent are deserving of our protection.

Many of the great leaders used this as a principle and accepted the necessity of using peaceable and amicable means towards building a stable governance and bringing about peace and harmony, while arriving at desired change in the society. Leo Tolstoy and 'Bapuji (Mahatma Gandhi) adopted the philosophy for bringing about the required change that totally rejected the use of violence and cruelty, yet at the same time kept a relentless pressure on the enemy to give in. Non-violent action (civil resistance) must be alternative to armed struggle against the oppressor and not as a meek acceptance of oppression.

Classic examples of the efficacy of Ahimsa (non-violence) movement are Mahatma Gandhi led movement spanning a whole decade as seen by the Britishers leaving the Indian shores and handing India back to its rightful owners. Martin Luther King and James Bevel adopted the same philosophy as they led a movement to fight for civil rights for the African Americans. More recent is the "Velvet revolution" of 1989 in Czechoslovakia that brought an end to the rule of the Communist government can be a very big win and a solid proof of the victory of non-violence.

Non- Violence Against Trees

Do plants have life? Do plants suffer? Do plants feel pleasure and pain? Do they scream when you clip or cut them? When these questions arise, it reminds us of the Indian scientist Acharya Jagadish Chandra Bose ("Physicist, biologist, biophysicist, botanist, archaeologist, as well as an early writer of science fiction"). He was moved by the way plants responded to being touched, or when disturbed, e.g., mimosa. The leaves would drop or become smaller in size or they would shrivel. He created the "Crescograph" to watch how and to calculate how they grow and move, in a measure as insignificant as being "1/100000 of the inch". He wanted to show to the world that plants have perception as well.

He published in his report in 1902, his findings: "Responses in the living and non-living". The report described the beauty of the effect of melodious music and "plant whisperings" on the way they thrive, as against the weak growth they exhibited, when harsh and jarring music/talk was introduced to them. Did you know that plants get into depression when they are in an environment of air pollution, and dark, dank skies Joy and misery is what plants experienced just like human beings do?

Plants can perceive the environment in which they live, and even "cry out" with certain very specialized sounds when they sense "anxiety" or "stress." We are not capable of picking up these sounds, as our minds are filled with thoughts and worries, akin to human beings. Plant community, perhaps bats and also mice, would be able to hear these sounds, and who knows, perhaps one day, a human being, who is in total harmony with his/her plant environment, might pick up these beautiful plant sounds?

However, modern scientist says, plants without a nervous system feel nothing. You need a nervous system and a brain. Plants are not known to possess a brain and neuron set; the way animals do. However, plant dies as they are living being. So, cutting down a tree is like a murder.

18

Joy of Giving

The measure of your life will not be by what you accumulate, but by what you give away". As human beings, we always find it easier to accept or to get something than to give. If someone were to give us a thousand Indian rupees or dollars, we would be so happy to accept. But if we were asked to donate the same amount for any cause, or to help a needy person, we would think twice, and may or may not give away the money. And we would usually have a dozen reasons and justifications for not giving.

To study well and earn a handsome salary, to live a comfortable life is the goal which most of us point out to our children. We are all social human beings. Man cannot live in isolation. So, society plays a very important role in nurturing our lives. It is our duty, when we become capable enough to earn our living, that we give back to society a certain percentage of our wealth for the welfare of the lesser privileged. God has given us the talent and gift and it is our duty to give back to God by serving mankind. It is not referred to as donation, but our responsibility and obligation towards the society.

It is very essential to return a portion of what we have so graciously received in terms of earnings or profit, to the society that has helped nurture us, for its welfare. Our personal as well as a group of individuals, we ought to deposit into society's treasury, that more individuals can draw out of as they evolve through life, to be the best they can be. Nobody lives in this life all by themselves because it is not possible at all. We owe a massive debt to the community we live in, in the process of moulding us. Giving back to the society ought to be an act of utmost joy. Here, it is important to dispel the myth, that one must be rich and affluent, to be a charitable person and give to causes. The very act of making an impact on another person's life in a positive manner is a mighty act. It is the little acts of kindness that make up the mighty ocean of happiness, wellbeing, joy etc.

But unless we give, we will never know the joy of giving. There is great happiness and pleasure in giving, perhaps even more than getting. What we get, we quickly take for granted, but the joy of giving remains with us for a long time. The Buddha used to say, "If you knew what I know, about the pleasures of giving, you would not have a single meal without sharing it with someone".

And to give, one need not be rich or materially affluent. If we can give money, clothes, or food to the needy, that is indeed good. If we are not able to give material goods, we can always give many other things that we have. We can give others our time, our attention, our services, our advice, our love, our respect, our knowledge, our experiences, almost anything of value is good. The idea is to "give."

Start with giving away something you really do not need and go on to other things. And see the feeling of happiness and satisfaction that you get. Giving also acts as a switch, to close the circuit and it is through this very closed circuit that you will begin to receive in quantities and amounts which are far more than what you gave.

These small acts of humanity and humility are to be instilled in our children from a very young age, at home, in our schools. It is a way of telling the children and the students that life is worth more than the CGPAs and millions earned. In today's competitive world, we spare little time for our children, to learn the greater lessons of life.

In the words of "Malcom Bane", "if you wait until you can do everything for everybody, instead of something for somebody, you will end up not doing anything for anybody".

We can start in our homes and teach our children, taking care of the medical and educational needs, of our maids' children; or helping women by educating them, in nearby slum areas. It can be anything, we just need to be aware and sensitive to the needs of the persons who are less privileged. When God gives us everything and a lot more, it is our social and moral duty to give a certain amount from what we have, after taking care of our own needs, for the benefit of the society.

Part IV

Sustainability for Co-Existence

"Our biggest challenge
in this new century is to
take an idea that seems
abstract ~ sustainable
development ~ and turn
it into a reality for all the
world's people"

Kofi Annan

19

Sustainability for Prosperity

Is Population Explosion at the Door Step?

When we talk about sustainable development, it always perplexes us into asking the question about the supporting power of our "mother earth". Will there be a time when our sheer numbers exhaust this planet beyond the point of no return? Several scientists believe that our earth has a holding capacity of around ten billion.

Harvard University's very popular socio-biologist "Edward O Wilson, has reason to make an estimate based on how much resource is there for the earthlings (inhabitants of the earth) to use. We have already touched 7.8 billion as of June 2020. This figure is according to the most recent United Nations estimates. The UN predicts, that by the year 2050 makes its arrival, the earth might have approximately "9.7 billion" human beings which might exceed 11 billion fifty years hence. The planet Earth is not a balloon that expands. Although there is an amazing volume of space to accommodate people, the space is not proportional to the resources of food and water, not to mention precious energy that is so essential for the survival of this huge mankind. Will this earth balloon burst with a big bang, for having been exploited too much? Will Earth be able to cope with the mankind's appetite for her precious resources? One study conducted in 2015 and published in the "journal of Industrial Ecology" has examined the effect of the environment from a very basic (viz household) point of view. The result gives us a startling peek into how much this is impacting: more than "60% of greenhouse gas emission" and "80%" usage of land, natural material, and water. What we need to wake up to, is make a change in us, starting at the individual level, by wanting less, using less of the earth's rare resources. This, and only this, will help make a lasting impact on preserving our earth.

What is required today is to imbibe the one of the fundamental spiritual principles of life i.e. Sustainable living (meeting present needs without hindering future generation's ability to meet their needs). We do believe that all of us will have to become leaders in sustainable development in our homes, communities, states and countries. To this, we need to take a vow to protect our mother earth with need-based consumption and by optimal utilization of resources.

Was Thomas Malthus Being Wrong and Even Today?

The challenges created by population growth and consumption based economic system have placed lot of strain and stress on our planet. These challenges have given re-birth to the philosophy of a British economist, Thomas Malthus. In 1798, Malthus very rightly predicted that human population will develop at a lot quicker rate than the supply of food until war, infection or starvation lessens the number of individuals. In other words, there is no proportion between the growth of human population and supply of food, because the first grows at a much faster rate, leaving a huge disparity. He mentions that there are two checks for population growth. One is positive or natural checks and the other is manmade checks or preventive checks. People will always face "civil wars" will starve during famine, or due to poverty, succumb to epidemics, natural calamities like floods et al. Malthus referred to these as "positive checks or natural checks" as these are the doing of Nature. We can, however, choose to have prevention which can be designed by man, or via "man-made checks" simple living, late marriage, self-restraint. His central message is that there is always something which prevents population growth and society is bound by ethics and morals to live up to the task, do whatever is essential, and ensure a disaster-free future. Whether Malthus was predictably right or basically wrong is a question on debate. Looking at the current trend of natural disasters and epidemic, the time is not far away to witness the validity of the theory of Professor Thomas Malthus.

Time to Protect Our Mother Earth

From Vedic lessons we have learnt "The earth is our mother, and we are all her children". So, it is our moral obligation to maintain the earth, our mother, adequately. The earth's survival depends upon the harmony between nature and mankind. Nature is fascinating, we all know that. We were so engrossed in ourselves and our living that we forgot to even give a thought for our future generations who would probably never have the chance to feel the tenderness of the natural world.

Human activity has been directly responsible for the climate change, biodiversity crisis and the scary pandemics of the past and the current one. Global economic system is dependent a philosophy that values economic growth, come what may. The only focus is higher Economic growth (with more output) by extracting our limited natural resources and motivating people to consume more goods.

Deadly outbreaks like Ebola, bird flu, Middle East respiratory syndrome (MERS), Rift Valley fever, sudden acute respiratory syndrome (SARS), West Nile virus, Zika virus transmitted from animals to humans. Human infectious diseases are growing at an alarming speed.

The outbreak of Covid-19 is a definite "wake-up call". We can easily say that human behaviour tampers with nature and allows diseases to contaminate humans. In order to check future outbreaks, man will have to make very conscious and earnest efforts: To stop deforestation, adapt-not destroy the natural world to boost modern agriculture, stop mining and put a full stop to eliminating the wild species. Human invasion caused this conducive environment in nature for diseases to wash over from wildlife to humans.

It is reported that Corona pandemic reduced pollution level across the world which was the biggest challenge since a few decades. Animals and Birds are enjoying open roads, highways, and water bodies without any fear. Many see the Covid-19 virus as a great disaster, we prefer to see it as a great "corrector". The Covid-19 has handed the golden change - opportunity on a platter, so to speak.

Scientists are foreseeing far worse pandemics, if we continue our wanton ways and ignore the protection of nature. The comprehensive 2019 "IPBES" (The Intergovernmental Science-Policy Platform on Biodiversity and Ecosystem Services) Assessment Report on Biodiversity and Ecosystem Services, forewarns that within decades, a million species are going to be studied under topics of "extinct animals and extinct plants". Close to two million unknown or not-yet-identified virus types cohabit with mammals and aquatic birds. Any of these might end up becoming more life-threatening and uncontrollable than the current COVID 19 virus.

We need to co-exist. We have forged an intimate bond with nature, unwittingly. If we abuse nature, we in turn, let ourselves down. As we move forward with a population of 7.8 billion and with a further population explosion, we better pause and plan and prepare a future, ensuring a strong merger with nature.

Vedas as well as the Upanishads teach us to look at nature not just as a resource to be utilised, but as divine life to be revered, and one that we can benefit from. From Dharmic perspective, greatest means of achieving sustainability is practicing nonviolence towards all, including nature. This will lead to harmonious interaction between human beings and the environment. Unless we reinterpret such teachings for the modern audience, they will remain confined to books. We need policies, systems and action plans formulated for the protection of nature, that will in turn sustain us.

The processes that are killing our soil, our biological diversity, our air, water and climate balance are also killing our humanity. We call it "Short sightedness". Rabindranath Tagore wrote in his essay Tapovan ('Forest of Purity') in the year 1909 "In the clash between extreme greed and empathy; subjugation and collaboration, it is only nature that can "impart peace of the eternal to human emotions". In 1922, "Gurudev" (Tagore) addressed students at Calcutta University on the subject of 'The Robbery of the Soil'. He talked about the importance of replenishing what you take from society as well as what you take from the soil. He conveyed that we are as much the children of the soil as of the human society.

Professor Stephen Hawking said, "I don't think we will survive another 1,000 years without escaping beyond our fragile planet." He also says that "Science should not be an elitist activity; it is something that should be driven by society for the benefit of society and we should aim for having everyone agree with that."

Raising awareness of our fragile environment & biodiversity has not been enough to solve ecological problems. There is urgent need for investment in sustainable and nature positive initiatives to be in sync with nature, for human and planet health. Governments must proactively fund for such initiatives.

20

Sustainable Management of Natural Resources

Sacred Groves · Spiritual Ecology

You might have heard of sacred groves. The idea of sacred grove has been adopted by various native communities all over the world: the Aborigals in Australia; the Kikuyu in Africa, especially "Mbeere" in East Africa; "Khanti" tribe of Siberia, not to mention native peoples in Germany, Greece, Rome, China, Japan and America.

More than 13,720 sacred groves in India, have been grouped, and they exist over an expanse of geographical topography and weather scenario. Basic rules prevent those living in the sacred groves, from cutting down trees and slaughtering animals. This directly results in conserving of biodiversity in these special zones. These zones' area can span from being a few square meters right up to several hectares. They have specific names based on their location: "Devray", Maharashtra; "Devarkand" and Siddarvanam" in Karnataka; Rajastan calls them "Oraans", "Kenkari", "Malyan", and "Yogmaya". In Chattisgarh refers to them as "Saran", Biharis call them "Saranya". However, in the tribal regions of Jharkhand and Orissa, they are very fondly called "Jaher". Kodagu's sacred groves, one per village and these are situated in the Western Ghats in South India. The presence of sacred groves seems to have been around for more than two thousand years.

When we talk of sacred grooves, it reminds us of our visit to Meghalaya state. In the year 2003, as a part of one consulting assignment for the state of Meghalaya, we had landed in Mawphlang village which lies in the eastern side of the Khasi hills. Since the assignment was develop tourism master plan for the site, looking at the forest near the village, it triggered our mind to explore developing eco-tourism in this site. While talking to the accompanying officials at the edge of the forest, they informed that this forest was an extraordinary one. The deity "U Ryngkew U Basa" that the village Chief and the elders reverenced, resided here. The deity would protect the village from all ills and suffering. Those who entered the forest with less-than-pure-intentions, would experience ramifications. "Law Kyntang", the sacred grove has existed for a thousand years. No branch of any tree or the tree itself may not be cut down, because it is an anathema. There are rare treasures of medicinal plants and trees found in this grove, make it so special. A village without a sacred grove is a non-entity. "Law Kyntang" has magnificent biodiversity.

Common Property Resources

Another aspect of sustainability is the Sustainable utilization of Common property resources which includes fisheries, grazing lands, forests and water. Ecologist Gaett Hardin in his paper "The tragedy of commons" has beautifully described the situation when public resources get depleted because of too many people try to maximise its return from it. For example, when the sheep herders shared a common parcel of land on which everyone can graze its sheep. It is fine as long as the sheep herders did not allow too many sheep to graze in that plot. But if a greedy herder brings in additional sheep, the pressure to the carrying capacity of pasture increases and eventually depleting the grazing land such that none of the sheep can graze.

Another example could be fishing in the coastal areas. Fish in open sea is a typical example of public property with open access.

Here it is more difficult to restrict access to public. Each fisherman has an incentive to catch as much as possible. Although the resource is renewable, overfishing will result and the resource will be depleted, which is not in the interest of anyone. Monsoon is the breeding season of nearly 300 species. To ensure sustainable harvesting of fishes, many Governments as a part of public policy ban fishing to conserve fish stock in sea during the breeding season. 'Fishing Holiday' is declared during the breeding period. This ban coincides with spawning (release of eggs) season. As trawlers and the mechanised boats use fishing nets with small gaps, eggs and small ones will be caught in the nets leading of depletion in fish production.

Interestingly, many communities in the world have shown how traditionally they can manage the common property resource with their traditional knowledge and wisdom through spirituality. These knowledge & wisdom transformed into cultural heritage, which passes from one generation to another.

It may not be out of place to mention here that UN recognizes "that respect for indigenous knowledge, cultures and traditional practices contributes to sustainable and equitable development and proper management of the environment." Making a policy and enacting a low will not alone be able to ensure sustainable management of natural resources. For example, the government of Nepal decided to nationalize all its forests in 1957, to put an end to deforestation and environmental degradation. Nepal government failed due to the difficulty in enforcing the law.

If we look back in the past all our recent positive development in healthcare, science and technology had an umbilical link with indigenous knowledge system in some way or the other. Even the philosophy, culture and tradition had contributed to our modern day's achievement. Traditions knowledge and wisdom forms the basis of sustainable development, a factor which is usually ignored by decision makers and even scientists.

Community's Love in Biodiversity Conservation

Another example of a community's love in biodiversity conservation is given below. There was bloodshed, in the "Khejarli massacre" whereby 363 Bishnoi community residents (who were peacefully protecting a sacred grove Khejri trees in a village in Rajastan) were culled by the soldiers of the Maharajah of Marwar.

The Maharajah of Marwar wanted the wood from these trees for his new palace, hence, gave the order to cut down the trees. This tree being sacred tree and a wonder tree of the desert area, the Bishnoi community from 83 villages fiercely defended the threatened trees. The elders were the first to go forward, were systematically massacred as they hugged the Khejri trees. Youngsters as well as women and children started hugging their beloved trees, and most of them were killed. 363 Bishnois laid down their lives in the supreme act of protecting their beloved Khejris. When the king heard about the killing, he was filled with a deep remorse, and ordered his soldiers to retreat. The king abandoned the plan of building the palace and the Rajastani people's fervour increased as they worshipped the Khejri trees. The Blackbuck freely grazes the area of the grove. Orphaned calves are nursed and animals that ail, are tended to by the villagers. Do we have a lesson to learn, from the Bishnois?

The environmentalist "Chipko movement" took its inspiration in part, from the Khejarli incident. The government of India has commemorated the day of the brave act, (11 September) as National Forest Martyr's day.

Water- Elixir of Life

If we look at all civilizations, human societies have all settled along the fertile river basins of great rivers like Indus Valley Civilization (Indus river); Ancient Egypt (the Nile river); Civilization of Mesopotamia: Iraq, Iran, Syria and Turkey, settled along the Tigris river and the Euphrates river and Chinese civilization along the Yellow river. Without water there would be no human civilization.

Almost 60% of human body is made up of water. Most often, we can go without food and try as one might, will fail to survive without water. Water is of such importance in our life, that water is called the "elixir of life". Currently, water as a resource is facing a lot of challenges, which if not met with serious effort from governments and people all over the world, will lead to a global disaster. The importance of water security can be seen from the fact that it is included as one of the goals in sustainable development goals 2020 by the UN.

We may find it strange because 71% of our earth is covered in water (hence the name blue planet). But 97.5% of that water is sea water, which is not fit for human consumption. Hence only 2.5% of fresh water from rivers and underground sources is fit for human consumption. According to WHO estimates 785 million people have no access to clean drinking-water. Globally, close to 2 billion people avail a drinking water source contaminated with faeces, Diarrhea, cholera, dysentery, typhoid, and polio are caused by the consumption of contaminated water and cause 485 000 diarrheal deaths years. What we need today is technology and innovations in clean and safe drinking water.

Another issue is meeting the demands of a fast-growing population. Just 2.5% of all available water is a serious challenge. Demand is increasing day by day because of increasing demand for industrial, irrigation and domestic use.

While talking about the of the planet's worst environmental disasters pertaining to water crisis, it reminds us about the case of Aral Sea, a lake between Kazakhstan and Uzbekistan. In 1960s, this had been the fourth largest lake in the world. About 35 million people were dependent upon the lake for water and fish. Now it has turned into a desert leaving a thin strip in the western edge. The climate of the region has changed drastically with hotter summer and colder winter along with increased dust storms and whole range of disease. This has happened due to over irrigation to promote agriculture and especially that of cotton during soviet era. The region's once thriving fishing industry has faced devastation, causing loss of employment and as a result economic decline.

The report published by the "Organisation for Economic Co-Operation and Development" (OECD), there will be 400-percent rise in water demand in manufacturing sector. 40 % of the global population will continue to live in "water-stressed" places by 2050. The report identifies groundwater depletion as the biggest fear, that will have to be experienced by the humanity. We mean groundwater as freshwater available from below the surface of the earth. Satellite observations showed that a majority of earth's water bodies, as many as 21 out a total of 37, drain at an alarming speed, but refilling is hardly proportional. This is all due to overuse of groundwater. Our water security is under threat. Various studies show that when it becomes difficult to reach water beyond 300 feet, it becomes an unviable economic venture for any individual or a company, to absorb.

A report by "The United Nations Educational, Scientific and Cultural Organization" (UNESCO) on World Water Development" confirms the fact India extracts the highest volume of groundwater (1/4th of the global ground water), in the whole world. This is greater than the ground water drawn by China and the United States of America combined.

To address this water crisis, the most important option is water conservation. If we look at the tradition systems of water conservation techniques prevalent in ancient India, they are all simple, efficient, and eco-friendly. Bawdi and Jhalara- Step well structures in Gujarat and Rajasthan, tanks in South and central India, check dams in hills are very popular. Karnataka has "Madakas" in Karnataka; "Pemghara" in Odisha and Rajastan has "Johads" which are the oldest known ground water conservation and recharge systems. Even use of rainwater and flood water harvesting was known since Indus valley civilisation time.

It is worth to mention one such traditional method called "Taanka." An age-old rainwater harvesting system is "Tanka" prevalent in the Thar desert of Rajastan. "Taanka" is nothing but a covered underground pit in the shape of a cylinder, which collects the water from the rain, flowing in from the rooftop, courtyard, or any constructed collection receptacles. When filled, the stored water can last through an entire dry season, servicing a medium sized family of five or six. A stroke of genius, for water security in these dry desert regions, a "Tanka" protects families from the hardship involving sourcing water from long distances.

We need to review and popularise these traditional systems of water harvesting. Are we serious about Earth and nature to readopt them? Further, it is the need of the hour to promote rainwater harvesting infrastructure and water recycling infrastructures at individual house and community level.

Fair Share of Resources

Currently, the world is faced with a dilemma concerning proper use of earth's natural resources. One, allowing a fair resource-use distribution and the second is the sustainable harvesting of resources. Sustainable harvesting refers to the harvesting of natural resources not faster than their rate of replenishment. Let us start with fair share of resources. As we are reach natural resource limits, fundamental questions about a fair share of natural resources are bound to arise. Global population is growing unchecked, and the people in the middle "rung" are becoming economically stronger. In the process, consumption of natural resources is growing exponentially. Accordingly, disputes over access to the natural resources like land and water are becoming intense.

Interestingly, the biggest problem in distribution of the planet's resources is equated to the unevenness of consumption, across the globe. The richest 20 percent world population that live in rich countries, monopolise a lion's share of eighty percent resources. This causes variation in climate that destroys the environment. The rest, of the eighty percent, the world's poorest have insufficient access to basics of food, clean water, and energy. Growing disparity causing poverty and conflict are a direct result of difficulties on account of climate change and depletion of resource.

How do we address this issue? This issue is an on-going topic of debate at the international level. Our dream of achieving a self-sustained world will remain a dream until and unless we step away from these patterns of production and consumption. When we respect Mother Earth and give her a prominent place in our agenda, minimizing commercial gain or exploitative economic system.

There is another perspective, even if a state/ country is resource rich, people yet stuck to poverty. For example, Jharkhand state In India- The first paradox of the state is that a vast portion of its population, lives in great poverty while natural resources-rich land, with forests, minerals, rivers, with abundant rainfall and fertile soil, fails them. Jharkhand makes up 40 per cent of the country's total mineral reserves but gives back only 10 per cent value of the country's total mineral production. The second is that, despite getting industrialised in 1907 with the set up of Tata Iron and steel plant in Jamshedpur and Dhanbad, boosted as the country's coal capital (over a century ago). The third paradox is that, Jharkhand, country's capital for coal, a mineral rich state (mica, manganese and bauxite) and iron ore, with two of India's largest steel plants:Tata Steel, the first private steel plant in Jamshedpur, and the largest public sector steel plant in Bokaro, it still comes at the bottom of the list of states economically and on "Human Development Indices" (HDI).

The reasons for this are clear for anyone to see: political upheaval, huge amount of corruption among the political elite in Jharkhand. It is a laughing matter to mention the fact that this state produced six chief ministers in 13 different regimes in a period of 16 years. Good governance with ethics and moral values of the society, government and business is the answer to tackle such issues. We may see lack of spirituality, sustainable approaches, and neglect to social interest by the decision-making segments, who are at the helm of power as a hindrance, to that attainable prosperity.

Sustainable Harvesting of Resources

Interestingly, the forest dwelling communities across the globe has demonstrated that with their traditional knowledge, they can harvest non timber forest produces with sustainable approach. The harvesters only extracted that quantity of produces to appease their immediate needs, so forests could regrow without adverse impact.

However, with the exploitive economic system, and the market demand for such produces, these communities have been lured to change the pattern of harvesting. Harvesters receive several offers in the market, to literally barter their produce for the current value. However, a lot of pressure is applied on the balance of forest resources.

However, many development organisations are working with the community to build their capacity to undertake sustainable harvesting practices with scientific approach. In this context, we would like to share our experiences while visiting one tribal area and interacting with forest community with Kovel Foundation, an NGO based in Vishakhapatnam working on NTFP project intervention in Visakhapatnam district of Andhra Pradesh. Kovel trains the gum picking community, and this has had double effect of reinforcing their livelihood and ensuring a superior quality of gum karaya, for export. The Kovel participators shared an improved practice of gum harvesting that they had developed. Their affectional hugging of the tree helps to measure its girth, those trees not easily "huggable" are classified as the right size. The blaze on the tree should not exceed 15cms and there should be no more than 3 feet ground upwards. Blazes should not be continuous. Use of forceps is preferable to the use of bare hands. Gum should be aired out on porous plastic sheets and eventually transferred to a basket to carry it. The whole process is very delicate and done with loving care. Very often, these careful methods are not practiced, which sees a premature demise of the tree. This experience opens our eyes to the challenge of treading gently without making an impact on dear Mother Nature.

21

Are the Pesticides Killing Us?

What are Pesticides

What are pesticides? Broadly speaking, pesticides include herbicides that kill weeds (unwanted plants), fungicides (kill fungi that destroy crops), and pesticides, which technically refers to the chemicals that kill insects. Pesticide residue is what may be left on our food, that is taken from the sprayed food crops. It refers to the pesticides that may remain on or in food after they are applied to food crops.

Why do farmers use pesticide? For a farmer, it provides higher yield. Higher yield is not in the true sense of the word, but the yield they would not have lost to disease.

Pesticides Use- Not a Modern Invention.

Pesticides are an ancient "ill". Farmers in ancient times also made use pesticides but they relied almost entirely on the use of natural products and preparations derived from those natural products. According to several studies, the ancient civilisations widely used extracts of lupine flowers or wild cucumber against a variety of pests. Greeks and Romans used smoke and protective seed coatings. They also used pesticides manufactured from chemicals and minerals naturally available in native soils, plants, trees, and animals. In the ancient India, there were using organic materials. "Surpala's Vrikshyayurveda" (medical science for plants in ancient India) mentioned some materials like milk & milk products, application of cow dung, application of liquid manure and practices that were supposed to be used in agriculture for the protection of crops. In other words, in the past, we have done farming without toxins and chemicals. Today the earth, our farms, our water, our food is poisoned and polluted.

Emergence of Chemical Pesticides in Modern World

The problem pertaining to pesticide started as agriculture has grown and industrialized. However, the Chemical age in agriculture started with the onset of World War II. Since then, farmers have come to rely on inorganic/ synthetic chemical-based pesticides for large-scale practices.

Just before the onset of war, DDT (chemically, "dichloro-diphenyl-trichloro-ethane)", The insect killer or "insecticide" had been discovered in 1939. It was then extensively used by the U.S. military at war times. The U.S. and other governments grabbed up revelation, researchers realized that typhus, carried by fleas; malaria, by mosquitoes could be eliminated using DDT. U.S. fighters were given DDT powder to sprinkle it in their camping cots and sleeping bags. Towns were DDT showered to dispose of lice. South Pacific islands made heavy use of it to eliminate mosquitoes. The word "DDT" became very popular with the view that "new miracle chemical" saved loved ones' lives. It is said that DDT was largely responsible for that decrease of death in war. It has been the insecticide with the largest use in the world.

Farmers also became very interested and wanted to purchase it very quickly. With the end of the war, farmers created a new chemical age. It was found to be extremely effective against both agricultural insets as well as human disease-carrying insects. DDT paved the way for chemists for the manufacture of other pesticides and insecticides. All the dangerous risks to human and environment were well concealed within the chemicals.

Harmful Effects of Chemical Pesticides

In 1962 it took Rachel Carson's book "Silent Spring" to awaken the world to the lethal effects of DDT on the environment, on humans and animal health. About 80 countries imposed a ban on the use of DDT immediately. This created a massive stocktaking on the impact of pesticides on environment.

Pesticides used in great amounts pollute soil and water reserves, and cause biodiversity to go out of balance. Pests too have their natural enemies in the environment, which are destroyed along with them, because pesticides do not discriminate which is necessary for the good of the earth. The staggering costs notwithstanding, impact the economy of the nations across the world. These pesticides leave a long-term effect on the crops, plants and eventually slither into the soil, and naturally contaminating water reserves in the ground. In the process, it poses a huge threat to the ecology and in turn cultivation of food. In other words, the entire food chain is affected.

Not only do pesticides endanger the ecosystems, they also cause related problems. One of the major problems with the over-use of pesticides is the development of resistance to them by the pests themselves, not to mention the weeds and diseases. When pests do not die, the surviving ones become resistant to the ingredient present. They lose their effectiveness eventually. What is worse is, the good as well as the bad are culled in one sweep, not sparing "lady birds", "dragonflies" and "spiders" who are the natural soldiers that safeguard crops from insects, because they feed on them. Pests thrive in the absence of these soldiers patrolling. Unwittingly, farmers increase the chemical dose in the spray, and increase the frequency of use, causing the evolution of weeds and pests. Repeated usage of strong pesticides, cause pests to develop a thick skin so to speak, eventually causing a scenario where nothing works on them. At least 25 strains of resistant strains have been identified by US scientist.

Producing newer versions and formulae of brand-new pesticides and releasing them into the market, is not taking care of the reason behind the resistance. With high concentration of lethal and dangerous chemicals, worsen the already existing problem, not to mention the high cost of covering this change.

Interestingly, nowadays the agro-chemical companies have shifted to "Neonicotinoids" or neonic, a unique type of pesticide that goes straight to the nervous system of insects and destroys them. Post 1990, these are being used on a large scale, with an argument that these types of pesticides are comparatively less toxic to mammals and humans. It may not be out of place to mention here that many of the insect species (like honeybees & bumblebee) which help with pollination are destroyed alongside. This is because honeybees like food sources neonic residues. Prolonged use of this type of pesticides leads to a reduced diversity of flowering plants. Imagine what would happen if pollination promoting insects were eradicated? Starvation on a large scale? If pollen-spreading insects did die out, it might prompt mass starvation on an extraordinary and unacceptable scale.

We may see a day when painstaking individual pollination of blossoms is assigned to batches of little people (children) carrying little containers of pollen paint and brushes. With the elimination of bees, we might lose as much as 71% species of crops that are only pollinated by bees.

Charles Darwin predicted the extinction of a few vital plant species, with the disappearance of the bumble bee. Albert Einstein said, "Remove the bee from the earth and at the same stroke you remove at least one hundred thousand plants that will not survive." Interestingly, a French publication on nature and animals, in the year 1965, announced Einstein's calculated prediction about the dismal "four-years" expiration period for the humanity in the absence of bees.

According to the report submitted to UN Human right council by "Hilal Elver, the Special Rapporteur on the right to food and "Baskut Tuncak", the Special Rapporteur on Toxics", "pesticides were responsible for an estimated 200,000 acute poisoning deaths each year. Some 99%, occurred in developing countries. Chronic exposure to pesticides has been linked to cancer, Alzheimer's and Parkinson's diseases, hormone disruption, developmental disorders and sterility" The report also states that "It is time to overturn the myth that pesticides are necessary to feed the world and create a global process to transition toward safer and healthier food and agricultural production"

Further, there are numerous studies which have indicated that chemicals such as "Chlorpyrifos" and "organophosphates" cause damage to brain function and are mostly directly responsible for causing pre-term births and neurological problems in humans. Endocrine disruptors cause low birth weight, abnormal brain development, increased incidence of cancers and reduced fertility among people living in and around agricultural areas. Pesticides that have been legally cleared for usage, contain disease causing poisons. The 2010 paper by the "President's Cancer Panel of US Government" concluded that pesticides are directly linked to several types of "cancers", which include "brain, pancreatic, non-Hodgkin lymphoma, myeloma, colon, testicular and soft tissue sarcoma." Killing people though cancer and pesticide poisoning is a crime to the humanity.

Agricultural chemical companies look only for profit, make big investments on pesticides, fully knowing that these pesticides are dangerous and harmful to man and his environment. It is important to mention that "we must not obsess with our habit of making short term profit at the cost of long-term destruction".

Is It Feasible to Avoid Applying Poisonous Chemicals?

One school of thought argues that farmers cannot save the crop without using these synthetic chemical pesticides. However, another school of thought argues against using it. Is it feasible to save the crop from pests without applying poisonous chemicals? Yes, it is possible. There are number of cases in India where non pesticide management programme has been highly successful. It would be interesting to discuss the case study of Non- Pesticide Management programme in Telangana state in India.

Non- Pesticides Management Programme

For Punukula, a small Kammam district village of Telangana state in India, cotton has been the mainstay in terms of a crop and had been monoculturally grown. Farmers relied heavily on pesticides for crop protection, however, the pests shot up in numbers due to spray frequency. The vicious cycle of borrowing money for pesticide purchase, seeds and fertilizers, paying interest on the borrowed money @ 3–5 % per month and their inability to repay these loans. They were forced to sell to the dealer for a lower than the market price, thus being caught between the "devil and the deep blue sea". High costs, selling at a lower price, debts, and the unbearable stigma of it, drove many a farmer to despair.

A fundamental change in the management of pests was imminent. The answer was "non-pesticidal management": that gets rid of pesticides altogether. Managing without using pesticide, includes many methods like:

- Light traps and bonfires which attracts moths.
- Fixing yellow and white sticky boards in the field, that attract and eliminate insects that drain the plants
- Meticulously picking out by hand, leaves containing insect eggs.
- Natural pesticides namely neem seed-kernel extracts and chilli–garlic extracts to get rid of bollworms and sucking insects. Other local plants also go to make natural pesticide.
- A mixture made from cow dung and urine on aphids and leafhoppers.
- Planting trap crops of castor and marigold to force insects to lay their eggs on these plants, and to then picking them off.

The end of the first year, saw positive results: farmers using conventional pesticides saw a huge loss, but the farmers using alternative natural remedies, made a profit. This encouraged more farmers to join in second year.

The village Panchayat council declared the village pesticide-free, for the future too. They requested pesticide dealers to refrain from coming into the village for marketing their products. The village farmers helped themselves and each other to become debt free in two years.

22

Industrial Agriculture System Vs Traditional Farming

Industrial Agriculture System

We all have presumption that industrial agriculture is promoted as a solution to hunger; we should also know that it is responsible for 75% of all health and ecological problems at global level. The industrial agriculture practice currently being followed by both the developed and developing countries has a hugely negative impact, namely global warming. Greenhouse gas emissions caused by fertilizer and pesticide use are the major contributors to the damage of ecology. Other than these two, fuel and oil (for tractors and other farm equipment) trucking and shipping (for transporting), electricity (for light, cooling and heating), and CO_2 emissions, methane, nitrous Oxide and so on also cause damage to the ecology.

We have already talked about the impact of synthetic pesticide. Now let us look at the impact of nitrogen fertilizer in our ecosystem. With a quest to increase more and more food production, huge amounts of fertilizer are utilized all over out the world. Of course, Nitrogen fertilizers have increased food yields thereby achieving self-sufficiency in the production in developing countries. Overuse of N fertilizers beyond the required limit, ended up degrading the soil, water and air. Prolonged use of ammonia-based N fertilizers, urea, caused soil acidity, in turn caused soil infertility. Crops now refuse to respond to further application of N fertilizers. Groundwater contamination of nitrate-N (NO3-N) is a health hazard to human and livestock, if its reading exceeds 10 mg L-1 in drinking water. The third problem is N2O gas emissions. This is 300 times more powerful than carbon dioxide, that result in global warming. So, there is significant economic loss which comes from loss of drinking water, loss of fishery and dead rivers.

What we need today is sustainable agriculture practices like organic farming, strengthen local food production system and limit the transport of foods to far way places.

Case of Organised Meat Industry

Let us start with livestock industry. Interestingly, commercial and organised meat industry is the cause of global warming. In a 2006 report, the United Nations said that rearing of animals for food generates greenhouse gases more than that produced by the cars and trucks in the world. U.N. Food and Agriculture Organization officials reported that the meat industry is "one of the most significant contributors to today's most serious environmental problems."

Let us take the case of Amazon rainforest, known as "the planet's lungs ", that produces 20% of the world's oxygen. Two of the industries involved in destruction of the Amazon rainforest are soya industry and beef industry. Although ancient farmers burned the Amazon, today's forest fires are very different. Today's fires are propelled by greed of money. In Brazil, cattle ranching is responsible for the forest fires. Trees are cut to clear the land for cattle pasture and this amounts to around seventy percent of deforestation in this forest. This is more than the area of Washington state. Chinese demand for beef is enriching Brazil's beef industry. Brazil, the largest beef exporter, promotes the expansion of this industry in the form of billions of dollars' worth in loans. USA alone imports 200 billion pounds of the meat. Although prior to this the biggest importers were Europe and North America, Chinese and

Russian markets gobble up more now. To meet the requirement of meat industry, Brazil exports a huge chunk of beef to China. So, the demand for meat from Brazil is increasing day by day.

Another important cause of Amazon deforestation is the expansion of soya cultivation by clearing the forest. The USA purchases the bulk of the soya bean supply from Brazil. 80% of Amazon soya is destined for animal feed. An alarming report by the "UN Intergovernmental Panel on Climate Change" (IPCC), warns us how drastic change in our diets will help 20% of the effort to keep global temperatures from rising 2°C above pre-industrial levels. This is something to ponder over.

Can We Ignore Modern Industrialised Agriculture System?

Modern agriculture is here to stay all over the globe. There is no doubt that modern agriculture has enhanced food productivity, but it has also accelerated several environmental problems: climate change, food being unsafe, biodiversity loss, soil degradation and environmental pollution (Zhang et al. 2017a). There is a prediction that global population will touch the historic mark of 9.5 billion by 2050 (Godfrey et al. 2010). By 2050, additional two billion mouths need to be fed. Can we do this without overburdening the planet? How to ensure a balance between food availability and lowering the environmental harm done by modern agriculture?

Modern scientists argue traditional agriculture cannot feed the world. Let us turn it around and ask: can modern agriculture feed the world? Those who favour modern agriculture support the use of modern mechanization, Chemical Pesticides, irrigation, fertilizers, and improved genetics to increase yields to help meet demand. Proponents of local and organic farming argue that the world's small farmers can achieve increase in yields and help themselves out of poverty, by adopting techniques that improve fertility without the use of fertilizers and pesticide. Both arguments offer much needed solutions; neither one is sufficient alone.

It would be wisdom to explore all the good ideas, from organic and local farms or high-tech modern agricultural system and take only the best of both.

Irrespective of the type of agriculture system, one country follows; we suggest that three steps are the need of the hour. The first one is using inputs (fertilizer and synthetic pesticides) more efficiently. Example-Application of synthetic fertilizer tailored to their exact soil conditions through soil testing and doing away with inefficient irrigation systems to replace those with precise methods like subsurface drip irrigation.

The second step would be reducing waste. An estimated 25 percent of the world's food calories, almost 50 percent total food weight gets wasted. In rich countries this waste occurs in homes, restaurants, or supermarkets. In poor countries wastage takes place in the transfer between the farmer and the market, due to unreliable storage and transportation.

The third step would be a change in food habit. A switch from grain-fed beef to meats like chicken, pork, or pasture-raised beef, will release huge amounts of food across the world. This is because today only 55 percent of the world's crop calories go to feed people, while the rest are fed to livestock (about 36 percent) for meat purpose.

In the context of modern agricultural system, the main problem of farmers is the increasing cost of market driven agricultural inputs (Seeds, Fertilizer & pesticides which does not make the farmers produce remunerative. In the process, there is agricultural brain drain. According to 2011 census of India, everyday 2000 farmers give up farming. Farmers are ageing. In the year 2016, the average age of the farmer was 50.1 years. New generation are least interested disinterested. According to a survey conducted by a non-profit organisation only 1.2 % of rural youth aspired to be farmers. We may ask why? Average agricultural household income is just INR 6,426 (90 US$ approximately) per month (source-NSSO, 2016). Forget a decent profit, farmers not being able to recover their investments for long (source: Report of the Committee on Strategy for

Doubling Farmers' Income by 2022). There is a huge disparity between farmers' incomes and non-agricultural professions.

Rediscovering Traditional Practices

Is it a high time to rediscover and re-implement traditional practices? Let the farmers be scientist. Let appropriate technologies be in sync with nature. Let the traditional knowledge be harnessed. Precise modern agricultural experiments are just about half century old, as compared to farmers' millennia old experiences. They cannot be made light of. Farmers' knowledge and technology are futuristic in nature, while being innovative, governed by ecological laws. But will organic agriculture or natural farming or traditional agricultural practices will boost the income of farmers?

Although the production may be lower than modern farming method, the reduction of the input cost, the market value of the organic produces found to be more than the market rate of conventional produced. So, this will offset the opportunity cost of additional quantity they would have got though modern method and also earn additional income. Further the organic produces command premium prices. Several studies have shown that there is huge demand for organic foods by the consumers from the health & environment perspective. Secondly it commands premium price. As a part of my academic research on the preference of organic food by university students, it was revealed that the students are ready to purchase organic food even if the price is higher.

Interestingly, a comparative study of productivity of organic and modern farming reveals that average organic farming produce in highly developed countries is 15% lower than conventional modern systems. In developing countries, it is 16% and in underdeveloped countries the average yield of organic farming system is 116% higher than conventional systems, (Te Pas and Rees, 2014). Regional variations are also present. E.g., small-scale coffee producers that converted to organic farming, saw a gradual yield increase of 15% in Mexico and 67% in Guatemala (Perfecto et al., 2005).

Similar, to Non-Pesticide Management programme (explained in the case study) both natural and organic farming are both chemical and to a certain extent poison free farming method. Both systems stop farmers from using any chemical fertilizers or pesticides on any of their agricultural practices.

We need to revive the concept of of rishi kheti (farming as practiced by ancient sages), the practice that allows nature take its course. In this context it reminds us the natural farming movement initiated by "Masanobu Fukuoka (1913–2008), a Japanese farmer and philosopher". He suggests dropping the necessity of a plough or any mechanised instrument, fertilizers, and pesticides for crop cultivation. He introduced the concept of 'natural farming" or "do-nothing farming". With no-till' technique, a farming philosophy demonstrated in Japan. This is well documented in his 1975 book "The One-Straw Revolution."

Fukuoka prefers to call a person embracing modern agriculture methods using chemicals, hormones, and synthetic feeds a "manufacturer" and not a "farmer". He was a man of science, a plant pathologist in Yokohama, in Japan. He was the outspoken and a strong advocate of the value of observing nature's principles. Fukuoka has shown the plant kingdom as an example proves, people know only a small part of the universe. More than 45 years after it was published, the book "One-Straw Revolution", continues to inspire us. Many farmers across the globe are following this method of food production. In India, this is being practiced extensively in Auroville in Pondicherry in India.

Like this approach, farming can be done with a zero capital, using locally available and farm-based resources. The farming principle is known as Zero budget natural farming (ZBNF) principles. According to this principle, plants get 98% nutrients from the air, water, and sunlight, the balance 2% comes from good quality soil rich in friendly microorganisms. (Just like in forests and natural systems). This concept of ZBNF was introduced by Subhash Palekar, an Indian agriculturist, who was awarded the Padma Shri in 2016.

The Government of Andhra Pradesh has implemented a plan to change over 6 million farmers cultivating 8 million hectares of land from conventional synthetic chemical agriculture to Zero-Budget Natural Farming (ZBNF) by 2024.

To talk about the interest of farmers on natural farming, we must talk about Vanrajsinh Gohil born in 1988 in the Junavadar village of Gujarat's Bhavnagar district in India. He says that Zero-Budget Natural Farming has doubled his income in just 6 months. In 2016, he reconnected with his long-lost friend, who is also a farmer, and when the two got talking, he expressed his displeasure with the use of chemicals and pesticides. So, his friend introduced him to Subhash Palekar, an Indian agriculturist, who was awarded the Padma Shri in 2016. A year later, Vanrajsinh registered for Palekar's organic farming classes in Ahmedabad. He is now working on his newly formed YouTube channel, where will post videos about his farming methods, he said "I want other farmers also to adopt the technique"

Climate Smart Farming

Nowadays the there is a debate about how necessary the enhancement of food production during the climate change scenario is. It has been suggested that traditional practices would be a noble choice for the farmers to cope up with climate change. "Agroforestry, intercropping, crop rotation, cover cropping, traditional organic composting and integrated crop-animal farming" can be adopted as the model practices of traditional agriculture for climate-smart approach. These are being practiced since generations.

Farmers in different regions have different and distinctive adaptation strategies with the change in climate. For example, farmers in Ethiopia and South Africa, use several drought adaptation strategies such as staggering planting and adopting new crop varieties. Sweet potato is a very conventional as well as food security crop that can withstand dry spell in South Africa. Similarly farmers in North-West Cambodia develop cassava which is a dry spell safe yield crop and can be developed in various soils requiring far less management.

In the Southern floodplains of Bangladesh, an indigenous method of farming called Floating agriculture is practiced. This is an exceptionally self-improved cultivating strategy in which crops yields and vegetables are developed on floating platforms (beds). These drifting beds are assembled using locally accessible materials, for example, water hyacinth and other aquatic weeds.

In Rajastan in India, there is Kachri which is a dry spell or drought tolerant conventional vegetable with short development cycles that can tolerate very harsh climatic conditions.

In India, with the facilitation support of an NGO named "Navdanya" individual cultivators in the state of Odisha, farmers have conserved about 1000 varieties of native Paddy, of these many are climate resilient like flood tolerant, salt tolerant and drought tolerant.

Community Seed Bank- Saviour of Genetic Diversity

It is reported that nearly 90 % of crop varieties have become extinct and around 75 % of plant genetic diversity pushed into extinction by the flooding of corporate controlled seeds. In order to protect the farmers from the problem of seed related issues, conserve the agro-biodiversity and protect them from the clutches of corporates, many development organisations in India have come forward to set up community managed seed banks. These seed banks help farmers become independent of large corporations and GM crops, help secure their access to local seed varieties.

One of such seed banks is promoted by an NGO Navdanya. They have established community seed banks by identifying and bringing on board, seed keepers / Seed producers in different agro-ecological zones of India. Farmers are imparted technical training on cultivation of these crops and raising seeds. These seed banks are managed by the farming community itself. Forgotten food crops such as millets, pseudo-cereals and pulses have been conserved which were pushed into extinction by the green revolution. At the end of the season farmers return the seed with an additional (25%) that they borrowed from the seed bank. These seeds are then given to other farmers in the next season to multiply and to enrol more member farmers. Till date Navdanya has set up 150 community seed banks in 22 states of India in the last 30 years.

23

Dilemma – Economic Growth Vs. Environment Protection

Are We Addicted to Economic Growth?

This year 2020, we are celebrating "50th anniversary of Earth Day", which was first established on April 22, 1970. The Covid-19 pandemic this year is a reminder that our existence on Earth is fragile," But this crisis is also a wake-up call, "to do things right for the future".

Every country is in a mad race for the economic growth. We are facing a dilemma. On the one hand, our current scenario calls for economic growth. On the other hand, increasing environmental pressures are bound to put severe constraints on the economic growth of the future. In the name of economic growth, money, and employment, we are totally disrupting our fragile eco-system. With a focus on growth at any price, billionaires are making billions by violent extraction of natural resources and using their billions to create markets and more money. Are the industries paying for the natural resources they are using? They are not paying. As per the recent report of the "Economics of Ecosystems and Biodiversity" (TEEB) program sponsored by "United Nations Environmental Program" (UNEP, it is a known fact that none of the world's top industries would be profiting, if they had to pay for the natural resources they use.

As per the World Bank report released in 2016, India had a setback of over 8.5% of its GDP in 2013, on account of the cost of increased welfare and lost labour, to air pollution. Considering the total GDP of $2.6 trillion, the loss equalled to $221 billion. If health and associated economic costs of water pollution are factored in, the economic loss is likely to be even more.

Similarly, in China deforestation had taken place on a massive scale during the period from 1950 to 1998 as timber was the backbone of construction industry. China's economic growth improved significantly during the period, giving employment to millions of Chinese. But it had negative impact also. There was economic loss of $1.22 billion annually on account of drought, flood, and other ecosystem factors. For every 1 dollar of timber sold in China, 1.78 dollar of ecosystem service was lost.

When we talk about limit to the economic growth, it reminds us 'The Limits to Growth" published in early 1970s by the Club of Rome. It warned us about the dangers and consequences. The message of this book still holds good today. We are still in denial mode. Even if the poor countries intermittently need some components of economic growth to reduce hunger, disease, and poverty, it does not become "economic growth." Let us at least use different terminology. Rather than the open-ended term, "growth," let us choose "sufficiency."

We need to re-think for a new way of life and live within sustainable limits. We need to re-think with a different perspective. How do we bring about new models of development, to achieve lasting prosperity for all? We urgently need new ways of designing economies for sustainability, transitioning to a resilient and sustainable economy. Can we think of Initiatives such as "Beyond GDP" or "Prosperity without economic growth? Or can we decouple economic growth and overuse of natural resources of the ecosystem? Which means economic growth can continue, subject to the condition of reducing the pressure on the environment. This may be possible with technology and innovations. We will discuss innovation later in a separate chapter. Again there must be an enabling government policy and actions for the same to happen. Time is ripe now to ponder over this issue.

Happiness Economy Beyond GDP

The wellbeing of our environment will always remain the focal component of humanity's happiness. Is it time to move away from Gross Domestic Product (GDP) to "Gross National Happiness" (GNH) or "Gross National Well Being"? When we talk about Gross National Happiness, we cannot avoid mentioning about Bhutan. Bhutan is a seldom travelled destination, but it is referred to as a champion in environmental progression. For 46 years, the Bhutanese government measures progress not through its GDP, but through GNH, with great emphasis on the protection of the natural environment.

GNH places people (and not material wealth) at the centre of its developmental values. GNH includes but is not limited to the psychological well-being measure (consists of life satisfaction, positive emotions, negative emotions, and spirituality), responsibility towards environment conservation (ecological diversity and resilience) and community vitality through relationship and sense of belonginess. The relationship among families and communities is based on trust, care, social support, and generosity. One study conducted by Harvard university in 1938 has proved that embracing community helps us live longer and be happier. It is the only and the first country to become carbon negative. It has also planned to achieve net green house gas emission to zero by 2030.

It is also worth mentioning about recently released first ever New Zealand's "Gross National Well Being" budget. The "well-being budget" emphasizes citizen happiness over economic growth or per capita income. In other words, the focus of the budget is not the country's wealth or capital in terms of its GDP but individual's happiness. The budget requires all new spending to go toward five specific well-being goals which includes fostering mental health and moving to a low-carbon-emission economy. These initiatives of both Bhutan and New Zealand will surely inspire the policy makers of other countries to seriously introspect and shift their focus beyond GDP.

How Bhutan Could Do It

Most countries produce far more carbon dioxide (contributes most dramatically to worldwide climate change) than they can absorb. Bhutan, however, is an anomaly. Ecological security is engraved in the constitution, which expresses that at least 60% of Bhutan's all out land ought to consistently be kept up under forest cover. Right now 72% of the nation is still forest. The nation has prohibited logging exports. Critically, the entire nation's power originates from hydropower. The nation has become a carbon sink. Being a carbon sink implies that Bhutan absorbs more than 6 million tons of carbon every year while just producing around 1.5 million tons. Bhutan exports greater part of the sustainable hydro-electric energy they produce from their river streams. This balances a huge amount of carbon dioxide. Bhutanese have a very high environmental awareness'" and "appreciate harmony with the natural environment. Bhutan even limits the number of visitors entering the country with a daily fee of $250 per person to ensure the environment is not spoiled by mass tourism. It stopped destroying their environment and started protecting it, something every country and individual ought to do.

Quest for Carbon Neutral Earth

Climate change is human made. We caused the problems, and we can also create the solutions. The solutions are there for the willing to use. The willingness comes from its wisdom and enlightened leadership. Several countries have pledged carbon neutrality. Like Japan by 2100, Canada by 2050, Germany by 2050, UK by 2050. Question may arise how to be 'Carbon Neutral' If you are not Bhutan.

To diminish the CO2 discharged into the air, nations need to utilization of cleaner automobiles, steer their economies away from carbon-intensive heavy manufacturing and change to clean and renewable of energy like solar and wind.

Green Business- Business of the Future

Nowadays we often hear the terms green jobs, green business, and Green economy. Let us explain the meaning of these terms. Green business organizations follow standards and practices and strive to make a profit without hurting nature (locally or universally), community, or society. It includes renewable energy, construction, transportation industry, biotechnology, agriculture, forestry, recycling, and waste management. Green jobs are those jobs in business that produce goods or services that benefit the environment or conserve natural resources. Creating green jobs is the only way forward, of producing decent employment with income opportunities. This would also address the problem of scare resources and ensure least harmful effect on environment.

The need of the hour is transformation of economies into a low-carbon, sustainable economy. We may call it "green economy". This green economy is certainly not a substitution of sustainable development; rather it is utilized as a vehicle for getting us to sustainability.

Green Jobs at sectoral and local level in countries like Kenya, Bangladesh and China demonstrate to us of the green business present opportunities. Let us give two successful case studies in Kenya. One of Kenya's biggest sugar makers "Mumias Sugar", rose to react to the high energy costs in the nation by going on an innovative green venture. Utilizing bagasse (a waste item in the sugar business), the organization could produce biogas that controls their power generators. Just 33% of the power it produces is used, and it offers the rest to the national network. This ensures good revenue as well as carbon credits. Moreover, in an offer to help local people and conserve indigenous trees and biodiversity, the organization buys tree seedlings from farmers and supplies them free of cost. Another Kenyan organization, named "Ecopost" utilizes 100% reused plastics to create aesthetic, durable and environmentally friendly products for use in fencing and landscaping. Ecopost created over Sh10.8 million in income in a year, saved more than 250 acres of forest land and has pulled back more than 1 million kilograms of plastic waste from nature.

The computerized world and the IT organizations make a decent attempt to limit the negative effect of IT operations on the environment. Planning, fabricating, operating, and discarding PCs and PC related items in an environment friendly are only a few measures. Green IT also involves overhauling of data centres, developing virtualization, cloud computing etc. For example, IBM operates a green commercial data centre, the biggest on the planet and with anticipated yearly saving of energy of 5B KWH. Their activities will bring about the reduction of 2.5 million tons of CO_2 every year, which equates to 1M cars not driven for 1 year.

Clean Energy

Another important component is the need for clean energy. The past three centuries of global progress since industrial revolution have made use of fossil fuel (coal, oil and gas) at the cost of the environment. Fossil fuels are used to make and power mobile phones, tablets, and laptops. It does not look like that our wants will diminish. Nor would there be evidence of a return to the days before fridges, gas cookers, washing machines and vacuum cleaners. The rate at which economic growth is going and the raising of living standards really began with the industrial revolution; this was made possible by exploiting of fossil fuels. Almost 80% of that energy at global level is provided by fossil fuels. Global temperatures have risen by almost 1C above pre-industrial levels, and there are more weather-related natural disasters. In 2017, 81 percent of the world's energy consumption was oil, coal, and natural gas. Nearly 15 billion metric tons of fossil fuels are consumed every year. Three countries China, the United States, and India use more fossil fuels than the rest of the world combined, making it 54% of the total fossil fuel weight, according to the Global Material Flow Database, by the UN Environment Programme.

The demand for fossil fuel is bound to increase further in the coming years. Sub-Saharan African countries are home to around 630 million people with no electricity. Apart from the impact on households, having no power to shortages in power are stunting their growth and job creation. Since new generations have, the aspirations for prosperity, without question, their energy consumption will go up. It has abundant reserves of coal – the most damaging of the fossil fuels. It is bound to encourage them to use the coal.

Teen climate activist Greta Thunberg addressed the World Economic Forum in Davos, Switzerland in January 2020 in 50th anniversary of World Economic Forum tearing down the world leaders at whom she pointed a finger of accusation "fuelling the flames" of climate change by their inaction. She said that simply planting trees was not enough and demanded an immediate end to all investment in fossil fuels. She said, "We want this done now. It may seem that we are asking for lots, and you will of course say we are naive, but we are actually seeking the "bare minimum" necessary to address the climate crisis facing the planet". She also said "Our house is still on fire. Your inaction is fuelling the flames by the hour, and we are telling you to act as if you loved your children above all else".

In fact, India is importing 75 % of its coal requirement from other countries. In the sense, the developing country is importing pollution to meet the economic growth which is leading to detrimental effect to the people indirectly. What do we want? economic growth or clean environment? Is it possible to couple these two seemingly contradictory objectives?

Do we not need electric bulb to be powered in every household? Yes, but with clean technology. Would we be able to envision a future that is cleaner, greener, and manageable without surrendering the economic development and everyday comforts to slide into decrease? The appropriate response is that it won't be simple, yet it is just possible if we make the correct decisions – and start now with commitment for meeting 100 % energy requirement through renewable & clean energy. Choosing of type of energy is based on competitive advantage of the industry. Therefore, the industry prefers to choose the energy type which is cheaper at the cost of the environmental hazard to reduce the cost of production. However, this type of competitiveness can be maintained by imposing universal carbon taxation.

Politicians and Government officials hesitate to do anything that is important to address climate change: they are in mad race for the economic growth, twist their knee to fossil fuel companies when these companies they request subsidies and tax reductions and are hesitant to back the potential of the renewable energy sources like solar power and wind power.

If we do not address this issue, the next catastrophe is just around the corner, and it is none other than climate change.

24

Re-Use & Re-Cycle

The amount of natural resources extracted to produce goods and services on the rise with the growth of economy year after year. A "hunter-gatherer society" had a per capita consumption of natural resources of around 3 kg per day. In agrarian societies, this rose to around 11 kg per day. The industrial society by the year 2000 started consuming 44 kg per day. As per the report produced by the "International Resource Panel" (IRP), part of the UN Environment Programme, Global material usage has steadily increased since 2000 and human consumption of earth's natural resources has tripled in 40 Years.

We often see, people with buying power, buy goods which may not be necessary but do so to show the affluence in the society. We need to be responsible consumer of goods and services. What we need today is to create awareness about the ecological impact our consumption pattern has, into motivating us to be responsible consumers.

For example: "to manufacture one kilogram of clothing, 27.6 kilograms of carbon dioxide is emitted; to manufacture a kilogram of computer parts, 96 kilograms of carbon dioxide is emitted". Just like how every food product label has a mention of the calorific values of its contents, packaged products and pollution causing services such as airline travel ought to mention the carbon footprint caused by the product/service consumption. In addition, school curriculums must educate children about circular economy (recycle and re-use). With a growing global population and growing economy, consumption of nature will also grow too, but we cannot change the size of our planet. How can we become more sustainable without renouncing the comfort of modern life and high-quality life? Recycling and re-use are two key solutions.

The first one is building up a network of multiple reuse centres, which gather, refurbish and sell a wide range of things, including furniture and electrical products. The second one is setting up of many 'recycling centres' the place individuals can bring a wide range of materials for recycling.

When we compare recycling, we find that while Europe recycles 70% of its consumption items, India recycles only 20%.

Therefore, there is tremendous scope for improvement, tremendous opportunities for innovations in the field of recycling. For example, French car maker Renault uses 33% recycled materials in all its cars in Europe. If a car manufacturer produces such results, it must be granted appropriate incentives by the government.

25

Social Responsibility

Environmental Offender Becoming Environmental Protector

With a focus on growth at any price, the business has been a major culprit in the earth's degraded ecosystem. These billionaires are making billions by violent economic extraction and using their billions to create market and more money. As Mohandas K. Gandhi said so eloquently, "There is a sufficiency in the world for man's need but not for man's greed."

But now many businesses are beginning to see how their survival is dependent on the vitality of nature. They need sustained natural resources, predictable weather, healthy employees, and prosperous customers. It is in their self-interest to promote sustainable business practices. Thus, a major environmental offender is becoming an environmental protector to the benefit of all.

Earlier, business houses accounting framework was on profit/loss alone. Nowadays business houses/ corporate as a part of corporate social responsibility are adopting an accounting framework with three parts: social, environmental, and financial.

Throughout the most recent 50 years, environmentalists and social equity advocates have attempted to bring the concept of social cost benefit analysis and full cost accounting for the company. For instance, if an organization shows a financial profit, however their asbestos mine causes a huge number of deaths from asbestosis, and their copper mine contaminates a waterway and the government ends up spending taxpayer money on health care and river clean-up. How do we justify this?

The business houses are also publishing sustainability report on regular basis. It is a report published by a company or organization about how their everyday activities impact the economic, environmental, and social responsibilities. Sustainability reporting can help organizations to measure, understand and communicate their economic, environmental, social and governance performance, and then set goals, and manage change to affect social responsibility more effectively. Sustainability reporting is synonymous with other terms for non-financial reporting; triple bottom line reporting, corporate social responsibility (CSR) reporting,

For example- In a first for the cement industry, "Ambuja Cement Ltd", a part of the global conglomerate Lafarge Holcim is one of the leading cement manufacturing companies in India. It adopted the triple bottom-line accounting method – encompassing people, planet, and profit. Its environment-friendly initiatives like the sustainable constructions and renewable energy projects have played a key role in India's efforts to become a green state.

The company was certified more than five times "water positive" in 2016. This was was made possible by providing a new life to used quarries by converting them into manmade lakes and building over 5000 check-dams to avoid water drainage from streams and rivers. Practicing sustainable mining, creating water bodies and development of pasture land have helped enhancing the landscape and biodiversity of the area around the company's sites. Today, 92% of Ambuja Cement's production is fly ash-based cement (Waste material of Power plants). Besides, the company managed reduced CO_2 emissions by 29% (from 1990 levels).

Many such corporations are working on such concept of accounting framework as their corporate social responsibility. But are all these being done out of compassion for nature or as a strategy for building reputation of the company for social responsibility and thereby for the growth of the company with the strategic objective of making more money. It is no longer sufficient to compete on quality, price, or product but the image of the company's reputation on social responsibility to win hearts & minds of customers.

Social Responsibility - Ancient Vs Modern Approach

Although responsible companies have existed for more than a hundred years, the term "Corporate Social Responsibility" originated in the mind of the American economist Howard Bowen in 1953. He then published it as "Social Responsibilities of the Businessman".

CSR has left a deep imprint in our cultural psyche. Many of us might have read in history books, how in ancient times, the kings (Maharajas) in India made donation of herds of cattle, horses and so on among other gifts to the people. Similarly, gigantic offerings to temples or religious institutions were meant for the development, employment, and shelter for homeless.

CSR is the effort to follow in the path of "Dharma. "The four" Shastras" according to Hindu philosophy, specifies four paths: "Dharma", "Kama", "Artha", and "Moksha". The individual's obligation to his fellowmen is Dharma. One of the main Vedas, the Rig Veda, gives instruction that wealthy human beings need to plant trees, to provide shade and shelter; and to build water tanks, to help the community; with the sure hope that their "afterlife" would be glorified. The holy scriptures emphasise the truth that the circulation of money to needy people is very vital as against the accumulation of it. Creation of wealth to see to the wellbeing of society is the foremost responsibility of business enterprise. "Atharva Veda" talks about acquiring wealth with fifty pairs of hands, only to distribute it with five hundred pairs of hands. The "Yajurveda" promotes the enjoyment of riches with a detached attitude. Wealth essentially belongs to everyone, and not to an individual alone. It urges human beings to enjoy riches with detachment, not to cling to them because the riches belong to the public, they are not individual's alone. Wealth ought to be shared among all, for the social betterment. Preoccupation in the modern way of life, we ignore valuable ancient practices. With the result CSR, seems alien to us. It is associated with corporate brand image building and PR practice. It has been delegated as less of a socially responsible activity. The few billionaires doing wonderful work e.g., "The Giving Pledge", founded in 2010 by Bill Gates, Melinda Gates, and Buffett, is signed by Mark Zuckerberg, Michael Bloomberg and George Lucas, among more than 170 people, from around the world. Bill Gates says "We think that's a basic responsibility of anyone with a lot of money. Once you have taken care of yourself and your children, the best use of extra wealth is to give it back to society"

India has produced several billionaires even as family businesses have passed down from generation to generation. One wishes there was a way to trickle down the wealth in a few hands to those in dire need of it. However, a few billionaires in India are doing extra ordinary work. Notable among them are Azim Premji and Tata Sons. These tycoons are the champions of humanitarian work in our country, with their monetary contributions towards the upliftment of education, healthcare, opening employment opportunities and much more. Azim Premji signed "The Giving Pledge" to donate at least half of his wealth, a campaign started by Bill Gates and Warren Buffett. Now Government of India requires those companies with a high turnover, to dedicate a mere two percent slice of their profit loaf, towards CSR engagements. This initiative by the government has propelled India into the position of being the first country to legally adopt corporate social responsibility on the first of April six years ago (April 1, 2014). With this legal mandate in place, many corporates have come forward for CSR activities.

COVID-19 crisis is a transformative moment for philanthropy. Philanthropic actions during COVID- 19 has demonstrated at global level that the corporate can do wonder for the cause of the society. Covid-19 has spurred an unprecedented level of philanthropy across the world already topping $10.3 billion globally in May 2020. In India, several corporations and their foundations like WIPRO, Tata Sons, Reliance Industry, Paytm, Adani Group, L&T, JSW Group have pledged to help in India's fight against the deadly virus. There are other companies that have also donated to fight against COVID-19 which include L&T, Infosys Foundation, Bharti Enterprises, NMDC and JSPL among others. Similarly, China's richest man, Jack Ma (Co-founder of Alibaba Group Holding,) has been distributing the essential "protestive masks as well as test kits, all over the world. He has also given 100m Yuan through his foundation to help fund vaccine development.

As Denzel Washington, an American cultural icon says "At the end of the day It's not what you have, or even what you have accomplished, it's who you have lifted up, who you have made better. It's about what you have given back." It is the ultimate truth, that the people who experience pure happiness and contentment, have been the ones who have given their best back to the society. They seem to be in complete readiness to exit this world, when "the call" comes for them. Their contribution would leave an imprint on the lives of others

What we need today is legal mandate of use of part of CSR fund for research and innovations to address climate changes and sustainable way of living.

Good Country Index - Index on Contributing to Humanity and Planet

We have heard of so many international rankings and reports that exist like Global Competitiveness Index, Global innovation index, Global Hunger Index, the Global Human Development Index, the World Happiness Report, The ease of doing business index, and all the others.

What sets the Good Country Index apart is that the Index is all about what nations contribute to humanity and planet for the rest of the world, rather than to its own country. As such, the most critical driver of a positive national image is the nation's commitment to humankind and to the planet, outside its own border and its own people.

Good Country Index has seven elements "Science & technology, culture, international peace & security, world order, planet &climate, prosperity & equality and Health & wellbeing". Interestingly, the Good Country Index has a rating for Health and Wellbeing, where India positions most elevated. While rating for Health and Wellbeing, they have estimated every nation's commitment to universal health & wellbeing related to the size of the economy, and not the provision and facilities extended for of health & wellbeing and prosperity to its own residents. Indicators used to rate this element are "food aid funding (according to WFP); exports of pharmaceuticals (according to ITC); voluntary excess contributions to World Health Organisation; humanitarian aid contributions (according to UNOCHA); and International Health Regulations Compliance (according to WHO)".

Curiously, on account of Covid-19, India has come out right on top in stretching out clinical assistance to more than 108 nations on the planet. Regardless of an underlying restriction on export of medicines, India lifted it to help nations battling with the emergency.

The European Foundation for South Asian Studies (EFSAS) report says: "India has taken a rather empathetic view of the crisis and has begun providing a whopping 85 million hydroxychloroquine tablets and 500 million paracetamol tablets to a total of 108 countries. It had initially banned the export of these drugs but reversed that decision as soon as it became apparent that the ban was out of place given the larger humanitarian challenge at hand. Little wonder then that world leaders including those of the US, Brazil, and Israel, to name a few, spoke highly of India's selflessness in this time of acute crisis".

Part V

Invisible Challenges

"Democracy is
"government of,
by and for
the people".

Abraham Lincoln

26

Big Data Controlling Us

Internet Became the Basic Need for Survival

We doubt if there is anyone in the literate world who has not heard of psychologist Abraham Maslow, and his theory of 'Hierarchy of Needs'. It was in 1943, that he brought out a report studying human motivation, that later became the famous Maslow's Theory of Hierarchy of Needs. As per this theory, a human being basically ought to fulfil his four basic needs before becoming the best version of himself/herself, in other words 'Self Actualization'. Those being physiological or physical needs namely air, food, water and so on, without which one cannot survive; safety needs come close on heal, as does personal security, the means of generating income, to enable owning of resources like wellness and comfort, and property. Inseparable to these two are the needs of love and belonging like close kinship, friendship and one's need for propagating to create one's own family and finally comes Esteem which comes in the form of a name created for oneself as well as the social standing in terms of respect.

Logically, scholars now feel that there ought to be a fifth need that has to be fulfilled, before arriving at that 'pinnacle' of self-actualization. "Internet", you guessed it right. The access to it, is seen as the fifth crucial need that is one step that bridges the basic needs and the best version of human self. Today, what gives your mobile phone that edge, is access to internet. Can one survive without it? Since 1990, internet has become an essential part and parcel of our life, be it in personal communication, in the education field, government machinery, in the business world, health and medical care, and not to mention aviation and defence field. We can almost see it as the catalyst that boosts social progression.

Internet today is the most vital aspect akin to human breath and denial of it seen as being very detrimental. The United Nations declares that online access is a human being's basic and fundamental right and offers provision of protection to this effect.

It is interesting to note that the protection of this basic human right has been taken with serious cognizance. In countries like Estonia, France, and Costa Rica, between the years 2000 and 2010, Internet laws have been passed to the effect of it being a basic human right. It will not be considered blowing it out of proportion to mention the fact that Finland has passed a decree stating that the internet speed cannot get below 1 (one) Megabyte per second (broadband level).

Data - The World's Important Resource

Just imagine a trans-Atlantic telegram, that ought to take only a few milli seconds, to transmit messages, taking several hours to arrive at its destination. This was nearly three decades ago. In those days, telegrams were very vital for businessmen.

Now data flow though internet is considered as the lifeline of global business. Data is of paramount importance in today's world and is the heart and the soul resource. Data and its widespread usage have made those companies that hold the helm of data control data have experienced mammoth growth and riches. To stay in power, now they want to keep governments away from data flow governance which we will discuss later.

Let us understand what big data is. Big Data is nothing but an electronic trail that we leave behind as we go about in our search for greener pastures. The tell-tale trail we create, a trail of our behaviour that can be snooped around, tailed, gathered, stored, and mined (extracted) through big data algorithms. These data give insights of our both personal and collective behaviour.

To talk about the data, we put into use daily is day is truly amazing. According to a report from IBM Marketing Cloud, 90 % of the data in the entire history of human existence has been created over a period of two years alone between 2015 and 2016. This trend of data generation will continue and may not stop.

In 2018 alone, data exceeding 2.5 quintillion bytes of data were generated daily. As per the report of World Economic Forum, the quantity of data generated each day is expected to reach 463 exabytes globally by 2025. Now it will be interesting to understand how big the Exabyte is. One Exabyte is equal to 1 billion gigabytes or 1 trillion megabytes (MB). Some experts have speculated that 5 exabytes is likely to equal of all the words ever spoken by humans. To have recorded one Exabyte of data, we should have started a video call 237.823 years ago. From this, we can imagine how big data really is.

On a positive note in the context of climate change and environment, big data generated by combining data captured via satellite imagery and artificial intelligence shall be very useful. This can be used to monitor forests, land use and harmful emissions and provide the answer of 'where, why, when and who' of the environmental problems. This may help governments, businesses, and landowners to pinpoint the exact source, the root cause and stop the harmful activities in the ecology. If the rich and developed countries can identify and monitor the military activities of other countries, cannot they find out the source and the environment offenders with the help of such technologies? There is a need for more introspection on this issue.

Interestingly, World Wildlife Fund (WWF) is tackling the issue of deforestation in the countries that are developing. Their initiative uses Big data and forensic science to deal with the trade of illegally procured wood that contributes to deforestation. With the use of Big Data, WWF is correctly able to correlate the data that links trade in illegally procured logs and their exports to countries which have a law supporting the ban on the export of logs.

Artificial Intelligence (AI)- Next Gen Technology Phenomenon

"Big data", "Internet of things" (IoT), "Machine learning" & "Artificial intelligence" (AI) have emerged as the next generation technology phrases, that we often get to hear of.

In the context of application of IoT sensors for positive social implication, it reminds us about our travel to a few villages in Mahbubnagar district of Telangana state in India. While interacting with farmers, we became aware that many of the farmers had availed loans from money lenders to drill bore-wells for irrigation purpose. But many of the bore wells did not yield water thereby their venture became unsuccessful. Since they could not repay the loan, many of them, unable to bear the yolk of debt, resorted to suicide. Reports state that from 1997 right up to 2006 alone, approximately 4,500 farmers' lives were lost to suicide due to their inability to repay loans availed towards boring of wells.

Let us discuss a real case study. Mr N. Rao (name changed), 26, a resident of Telangana's Mahbubnagar district committed suicide. He had bought half a hectare (ha) of land for paddy crop. His loan was 1.5 lakh to sink three bore wells and was unsuccessful in finding groundwater. His loan amount was used up and he was unable to repay the debt, so he hung himself in his house. After his death, his wife, along with their four years and two years' old sons, left the village to move to Hyderabad city in search of work.

We wish this technology would have been available to them: IoT Agriculture Sensors to determine the level of groundwater and soil moisture data to enhance crop conditions, increasing efficiency and crop yield. Mr. N Rao's life as well as those other farmers' lives would have been saved.

Undeniably, this technology has lot of positive impact on our society now and will continue to benefit our modern world in the time to come. Negative consequences are inevitable and seem dangerous as well. Artificial intelligence is after all artificial, not innate and it follows logic and a complex set of rules and instructions. AI cannot use wisdom for decision making, choices and actions. Morality or fairness is a non-entity in a machine that works automatically. It does not have a conscience. In other words, it cannot feel pain or suffering. Secondly, it may have serious impact on the job market by displacing human effort and thereby increasing unemployment.

It is but right to mention the Physicist Stephen Hawking's most worrying and warning statement "Success in creating effective AI could be the biggest event in the history of our civilisation or the worst. So, we cannot know if we will be infinitely helped by AI, ignored by it and side lined, or conceivably destroyed by it."

Great Risk -Big Data Watching us

Whenever we talk of big data, the most initial alarming factor comes to our mind is the public access to our privacy, as most private entity of our life, be it where we live and work, what we buy and what interests us is monitored by the mobile devices. Online shopping, and what we browse through on the web is not our business alone, not just that, it gets recorded and shared among who knows how many entities? As if it is not easy enough to find where we live and where we go, these entities make it their business to know who we love, how we live, and what we think. In other words, we can say that big data is watching us.

Currently people are ready to share their personal data with the exchange of free e-mail services, downloading mobile application or funny videos. At a later period, ordinary people might find it difficult to block the flow of data. There is growing consensus that like the two sides of a coin, big data comes is a great opportunity, but comes with a great risk. We often ignore the dark side.

Technology companies have already started their efforts to keep the government away from data flow governance. "The Internet Association", a major lobby that represents internet companies, a few that surface to the mind being "Google", "Facebook, and other giants, is leading the effort to prohibit governments from regulating data flows. If governments bow down, big data, the world's gigantic resource will be in the hands of the powerful private companies and the rest of us will be left in the dark wondering what really happened, powerless to even influence the steps that impact our lives.

Our minutest moves can be detected and studied. Everything, all encompassing. Sensible people refrain from sharing information about their family and children. We are not privy to stuff like our health, our purchasing behaviour, and our social life. Is it right to track information shared by others, and who decides the right and the wrong of it? Who is the rightful owner of people's private information and how, when and what do they access it for?

Talking about data risk, draws our attention to the scandal that broke out in the year 2018. We wonder if everyone is aware of the details of it: how two major newspapers of the USA exposed the story of a political consulting firm "Cambridge Analytica" that gathered information of over 87 million Facebook users, of course without their consent. What is interesting is what they did with this goldmine of data. It was purchased by the Trump campaign in the USA, used it for their election campaign in 2016, by having messages directed at the Facebook users.

Further, information gathered could be used for spying on us. It has already started. China has developed a "social credit score" for rating of citizen based on the data of all aspects of life including judging citizens' behaviour and trustworthiness. The rating is influenced by what an individual shares and how they behave, not to mention what your friends share and do too. Incidentally, it is no surprise that Russia's "Red Web" is most certainly a back entrance to the web world, giving full access to the intelligence agencies to every individual Russian ISP.

Can we live without Google and Facebook (currently owner of WhatsApp and Instagram)? These two companies have enslaved us. Just because we invented a powerful technology does not necessarily mean we have to be enslaved by it. Recently, one study conducted by researchers at the Oxford Internet Institute shows the different ways, people are trying to use social media with the help of big data to manipulate public opinion across nine countries. These are the Big Questions that Big Data is forcing us to confront.

Human Consciousness Vs Artificial Intelligence

One of the important components of the digital revolution age is the merger of biotechnology and information technology. This has the potential to not only transform our economy and society but also our bodies and mind. In this process, it may distort our mental system. With the merger of biotechnology and information technology, increasing amount of information will be transmitted from our personal biological and intellectual entity to artificial intelligence machines using biostatistics sensing devices. Subsequently with the big data generated, the private companies and government will be able to manipulate our mind and make decisions on our behalf.

There could be a dangerous impact on humanity. We can say big data manipulation may lead to an Intellectual slavery. How can we prevent a small group of elite people from controlling our mind? Do all these data belong to me? Will a Private conglomerate or the Government be the custodian of the data? If it is government, politicians may press our emotional buttons directly generating anxiety, joy, and hatred at their will and sell their ideology to us.

The revolution of big data technology may create a different type of dictatorship. We may call it a digital dictatorship in which all power will be concentrated in the hands of a few elite. Yuval Noah Harari's book "21 lessons for the 21st Century" remarked that "In the coming century, humans and machines might merge so completely that human will not be able to survive at all if they are disconnected from the network"

Despite the immense power of AI, its usage will continue to depend on human consciousness. The real danger is that we are investing too much in developing AI of computers but too little in developing human consciousness. To avoid the drastic outcome, it would be wise to invest in advancing human consciousness.

Currently, the exploitive economic system would provide the marketers incentives to sell any goods or services, even if it is harmful to the ecology and humanity, but it gives us zero incentive to expand our consciousness and compassion for the planet and humanity. We are not fully aware about the potential of human. We know very little of the human mind. If we are not careful, we will end up wreaking havoc in the society.

27

Global Inequality is on the Rise

What do we want - Prosperity or Inequality?

While talking in-equality, we remember our college days. When we joined colleges, we were attracted to the idea of a world of equality and a class-less society and then we came across the quote of Karl Max "From each according to his ability, to each according to his needs". With the collapse of Soviet Union and the shifting of Chinese communist regime's ideology towards more capitalism without democracy, we can say that Marxist ideals of equality are not suited to the current world. Then does it mean that capitalism is a solution to address this inequality?

To begin, let us look at the recently published report- "The Davos report 2019 -Public Good or Private Wealth?". It clearly emphasises that despite economic growth, tens of thousands of people continue to live below the poverty line, while a lion's share of wealth is accumulated at the very top of the pyramid. As per the UN report, more than one and a quarter billion people are still "multi-dimensionally poor", which goes to show that poverty is not merely of money or income, but also of malnutrition and ill health, less than acceptable nature of work, lack of proper sanitation, lack of security, and more importantly lack of education.

A few countries like India and China have uplifted millions of people from poverty. India lifted 271 million people out of poverty over a period of 10 years between 2006 and 2016. India and a few neighbouring countries like Bangladesh and Pakistan as well as some far eastern countries, a few African countries as well as some South American countries have been successful in uplifting people from multidimensional poverty. Despite improvement in some countries, the trends are not encouraging at global level. Our economic system is based upon an assumption that with the growth in economy, we can create wealth in the system and poverty among people can be simply eliminated. Is it possible to achieve this without addressing the inherent issue of re-distributing wealth? Despite the economic growth, poverty still exists, and the in-equality is rising year after year. Let us look at the Credit Suisse Global Wealth Report 2019. According to this report, the world's richest 1 percent, own a lion's share of 44 percent of the whole pie (World's resources). In the past year, every couple of days, a new game of creating a new billionaire is being played. There exist more than 2000 billionaires in the whole world. The 1900 billionaires have a knack of increasing their wealth by a dozen percent. On the contrary, the other half, who are the poorest, approximately 3.8 billion numbers of people, saw in dismay their pittance (it is an insult to call this wealth) sliding steeply by 11%. Wealth is being controlled just by the super-rich. In 2018, 26 super rich and famous owned as much wealth as the rest of the other half, the forgotten 3.8 million. Have you seen the size of the current day playgroup rooms? Visualise this, a room full of playgroup "Richie" kids have control over wealth equal to half the planet's population. Strange though it might sound, but it is believed that Jeff Bezos (the world's wealthiest man also the owner of Amazon) could fund the health and nutrition budget allocated to the 115 million Ethiopians with a handful of peanuts that is just a percent of his wealth.

The report that Oxfam brought out, states a fact that we are no strangers to: Inequality which has always been prevalent, is seeing a sharp rise in the last thirty years. The super-rich have bagged the biggest chunk of wealth amassed through inheritance and patronage capitalism. 77% of the total national wealth is in the treasury of just ten percent of population. In the last decade, the number of billionaires at the global level has nearly doubled. Can this boom in billionaires, and the meteoric rise of "Filthy rich" (as a term goes), be harmful to the society? Need to ponder over this.

Another recent Oxfam study showed how politics has been monopolised by the super-rich in Latin America, India, South Africa, and other countries. Many of today's new breed of politicians are either super rich themselves or have substantial financial support from super-rich. If we examine the relationship between inequality and politics across the globe, we can find a trend. In every political system, including democracy, the rich automatically tend to lean toward control of political power. The agenda is crystal clear, that this political power is used to promote policies in turn backing the economic power of the rich elite. The scales tip towards the rich and a steeper inequality is created. Surely, we are sure to move away from democracy toward society governed by the wealthy or elite. It is said that "every billionaire is a policy failure," and that to end poverty and build fairer societies, we have to scrap the idea of extreme wealth. Is it prosperity? Prosperity comes from equality and education and not from the pursuit of more and more inequality. Increasing in-equality is a disturbing trend.

Can We Escape from Inequality?

Inequality is bound to exist, as all cannot have the same income due to the fact that our efforts and results may vary and sometimes a few things are not in our control too. Some call it luck. The only condition by which inequality can be accepted: if it supports the interest of the bottom of the pyramid population and it ensures that it raises the economic stature (income) of the poorest of the poor. If this trend of increasing in-equality continues, the economic system may collapse. It is not the absolute level of income or poverty that is the issue, it is the degree of in-equality which is a big problem. The absolute wealth or income is not the proper indictor of measurement of social progress but the relative in-equality in our society is the real indicator of social progress, Of course complete equality is unfair and the complete in-equality is also unfair. Wilkinson and Pickett in their book "The spirit level" argue that everyone is affected by inequality of income. Their case study states that income inequality is directly proportional to a range of health and social issues. They have demonstrated this via the data used from the 24 richest countries in the world. They have stressed the fact that people are significantly worse off in more unequal societies in countries. However, in more equal socio-economic societies, people at all levels of the social hierarchy do better and are happier.

We need to find a fair limit of minimum and maximum income. Then a question may arise. What is the proper range of in-equality? It may sound strange but the best way for the high income group of people to upgrade their own lives is to help support improvement in the lives of those earning less than them by sharing wealth or to help build the capacities of the poor to earn better.

If we examine the relationship between wealth inequality and political scene across the globe, we can find a trend. In most political systems, that includes democracy, more political power is partial to the rich. The real danger is that this political power is used is to promote policies that promote the economic power of the rich, once again tipping the scale of inequality. So rich becomes richer and poor becomes poorer. As inequality increases, we run the risk of deviating from democracy. A new order or a society governed by the wealthy or elite is born. We slowly edge towards a new order of government that is "Government of the People, by the Elite, for the Rich"

28

Who is More Powerful – Government or Corporations?

Monopoly Power of Corporations

With globalisation, the Corporations have so much power and control over every aspects of our life. Corporations have become a remote controller. We may be astonished to know that the revenue of a few global corporations is much higher or at par with the economy of some of the largest countries in the world. For example "Walmart's" revenue (514 billion US $) exceeds the total revenue of India (380 Billion US $), South Korea (251 billion US $), Australia (485.2 billion US $). Interestingly, as per the latest survey on revenue generators, of the top 100 globally, 71 are global corporations and the remaining are governments.

Familiar with Nick Shaxson's book, "Finance Curse"? In it, he describes the way in which a few private companies have complete monopoly control of most of the sectors of our global economy. Be it food, agriculture inputs like seeds, fertilizers or pesticides, pharma companies, the print and internet media, finance, or technology, every sector is controlled fully by a select group of "elite" (corporations). Business has become more powerful than governments

In a span of four decades, more than 30 agricultural companies have merged into the mega three by 2018: Dow-DuPont, ChemChina-

Syngenta, and Bayer-Monsanto. Today, these three companies control most of the global seed market, leaving only 30% to the rest of the globe and in the case of the pesticide market, they leave even less, only 25%. So, the pesticide and seed industry control are completely concentrated in a few mega-corporations. Farmers are left with far fewer choices to juggle between food production and higher prices, and it all goes to show that power is handed on a silver or golden platter to these Corporations.

The dominance of these few giant corporations is likely to control the entire agriculture and food sector and even the most basic sustainability rights including the right to food, water, and livelihoods. We will be astonished to know that, with the flooding of corporate controlled seeds, almost 90% varieties of crops have become extinct which is the same fate that is being faced by 75% of plant genetic diversity.

Crisis of corporate control over our food production is one of the biggest catastrophes we are facing now besides the climate crisis. If the corporations have their dictation and monopoly control, our life will be painful; the diversity of species will be driven to extinction. People may lose their freedom to select seeds, to their food, their knowledge. In the process, our decision making as well as all social relations may get disrupted.

People have already started losing their freedom to select seeds and are enslaved with the monopoly control of such global corporations. This is best explained with the recent example, how PepsiCo initiated the legal proceedings against poor potato farmers in Gujarat in India, alleging that the farmers are illegally growing PepsiCo's patented potato seed variety. The company had registered the seed variety as an "Extant Variety" with "Protection of Plant Varieties and Farmers' Rights Act" (PPVFRA). The "extant variety" means the variety of potato was already available and existed in the country when PepsiCo registered its seed. Even though, the potato farmers were not necessarily using the same PepsiCo variant, they become victims at the hands of the giant corporation. Although PepsiCo later withdrew the cases against them after the farmers had to sign an agreement with PepsiCo that they would purchase the seeds from PepsiCo and then produce and sell it on PepsiCo's terms and conditions.

Similarly, Monsanto's monopoly control of the world's food supply with its proprietary seeds and genetically modified organism is explained with the example of Monsanto company (now Bayer) "Bt" variety of cotton seed. The company has so deeply penetrated in India that about 90 % of cotton cultivation in India is done with Monsanto's Cotton variety of seed. They had been charging exorbitant price of cotton seeds to farmers in the name of "Bt 2 trait" (seeds providing immunity to the plant from pest pink bollworms). Interestingly, the premium is charged to farmers, with a claim that it is patented. Such patents, which they claim, have now expired, and are deemed illegal in India. Now the government of India, to protect the farmers from exorbitant price of cotton seeds, is intervening in the price -fixing a maximum sale price for the "Bollgard-II (BG-II) cotton seed".

Another important aspect, we need to investigate is the dependence of farmers on these companies. Monsanto introduced I st Generation "Bt Cotton" Called "Bollgard-I" and thereafter second generation "Bollgard-II". They claim that these provide immunity from pests like bollworms to the cotton plants. It is reported that about 80 % of the cotton growing areas are now infested with bollworms. Bollgard 2 or BG-2, Monsanto's second-generation insecticidal technology had claimed protection against the pest pink bollworm, as every virus or pest, they have developed resistance to the toxic strain that the plant has grown. As a result, farmers now spend more on pesticides to control infestations. Coupled with the high cost of Bt seeds, farmers fall into the debt trap. The other option the farmer has, is to depend on the company for the third generation- BG-III cotton seed. Either ways, farmers are getting into a trap with the monopoly control of such global corporations.

Government Competing with Corporations

The power of government has not disappeared. Interestingly government is now competing with corporations for influence and power with a nexus. Government wants revenue, policy and law makers want favour and business wants profit maximisation. Nowadays, the business houses through their own think tanks or political funding, lobby with the policy makers to influence them to get favour for the industry/business. It is reported that, in 2017, Google dedicated a budget of over US$18 million, lobbying politicians and lawmakers, thus rising to the position of # 1 lobbyist in the world, while Facebook spent a slightly lower fortune, but nonetheless US$11.5 million.

Let us take the example of alcohol industry in India. The truth is that state governments are increasingly dependent upon the revenue brought in by the alcohol industry, to meet with their expenditure. About 20–30 % of most State governments' revenues are funded by the taxes brought in by alcohol sale. This share is going up every year. Therefore, government will always be interested to get higher revenue either though increase in consumption volume or increase in tax. On the other hand, the businesses are interested to maximise profit either by higher sales volume. During COVID- 19 lockdown, with the pressure of industry bodies and the need for revenue by the cash strapped government, many state governments of India introduced door delivery of alcohol drinks.

It is reported that to serve the people, state governments are compelled to encourage sale of alcohol and thereby mobilise funds. It would be interesting to note that the state government of Gujarat, India, has not mobilised a single penny for last sixty years through alcohol sale. If Gujarat, one of the developed states in India, can serve people without mobilising fund from alcohol sale, why not other states? Or are we missing an invisible formula in Gujarat?

National Institute of Mental Health and Neurological Sciences, NIMHANS, study in Karnataka a few years ago, found that for every rupee the government got off the sale of an alcohol bottle, it lost double that through healthcare expenses and lost productivity. So, both these entities are depended on each other for their own benefit, at the cost of the society.

Let us take another example of how tobacco-industry lobbies with government policy makers. Three experts, two of them British, Nicholas S Hopkinson and Martin McKee and K Srinath Reddy published a paper published in the 'British Medical Journal' which states that: "In October 2014 the Indian government had announced plans to mandate the use of pictorial health warnings covering 85% of tobacco product packaging, which was to come into effect from 1 April 2015. However, a committee of parliamentarians that had consulted tobacco industry lobbyists, successfully recommended that these plans be suspended. Although tobacco is estimated to account for 40% of all cancers in Indian men, the committee chairperson made the extraordinary assertion that no study in India had established that tobacco causes cancer". To address these challenges, the clear value system of business leaders and business executives with moral values, business ethics and compassion are the ardent needs of the hour. We will discuss about business ethics later. Tackling such mindset can be only possible with spiritual revolution.

Government's Geopolitical Goals Through Corporations

It is necessary to make a note, at the global level, governments are making use of corporations as puppets as a means to an end, to achieve geographical as well as political goals. Powerful corporations are getting very aggressive in their strategies to maximise profits in turn. We need to recognise that the global corporations are no more bystanders but are political actors. This is demonstrated by the recent meeting between President Donal Trump of USA and the CEO of Apple corporation, Tim Cook, where the agenda was the strategize a trade war with China to benefit the interests of Apple.

Government owned corporations are the other component in the recent growth spurt. Almost one quarter of the Fortune Global 500 are controlled by these government owned corporations. We can call these global corporations as translational state-owned corporations. These companies have started investing outside of their geographical parameters and gain strategic leverage via other countries or players. For example, many state-owned Chinese companies have increased their investments in Africa to secure a solid base of raw materials to fuel its economy and to wield its global political dominance.

This reminds us how in 17th century, Imperial powers used the corporations to maintain all compassing control of trade monopoly, amassing resources and capturing territory in some of the biggest continents, namely Asia, Africa, and the Americas. East India Company made its massive presence made known and further expanded into a vast enterprise, conquering India with a totality of trade dominance ownership of territories and the right of government power. At its pinnacle of power, the East India Company had a total control over the Indian population, that is equivalent to a fifth of world's total population. All that with a army of a mere quarter of a million. If this is what we are heading towards, it may have a different world order with more exploitive economic system.

Public Private Partnership (PPP) for Development

The government and private businesses should not collaborate to create only the wealth of private sector. They can come together and collaborate to provide public infrastructure and service delivery in multiple sectors like transport, water supply, healthcare, energy etc. through public private partnerships (PPP). Thereby it can play a vital role in bringing about a sound socio-economic balance.

Currently across the globe, there are multiple examples of successful PPP initiatives. In India, there are several success stories where projects were well implemented in the sector such as in roads, ports and airports.

However, there are multiple examples of failure cases also. The reasons for failure could be due to multiple factors including not being able to manage various risks involved in the project.

However, we must accept the fact that the objectives of government and private sector are contradictory in nature. The private sector will always strive for maximisation of profit and the government's role is welfare of the citizens. Therefore, what we need is strong PPP regulatory mechanism so that primary objectives of partnership are achieved with win-win situation for both government and private.

29

Does Media Controls How We Think?

Media Serving Whose Interests?

As an individual and society, currently we are hypnotised and programmed by media and the market. We need to understand who is behind hypnotising us and why we are succumbing to it. There is no doubt that the media has the power to influence our thoughts and actions. The methods used to convey the information are naturally hypnotic; concentrating our attention on a specific item with repetition, forcing us into reducing attention that we give to everything outside that focus. We can say that media is an important tool to reprogram our subconscious mind.

In order to cater to the requirement of linguistic diversity in India, there is vast number of media outlets. A recent data as of 31st March 2018, over 118,239 publications were registered with the Registrar of Newspapers, out of which more than 36,000 are weeklies. Over 550 FM radio stations prevail in the country as well as, more than 880 satellite TV channels out of which 380 of them claim to broadcast news and current events. Interestingly, it is impossible to measure the number of news websites operating in India.

Despite the vast number of media outlets, the production of media content and its distribution is undeniably in the control of a few chosen elite. The media ownership rests in the hands of a certain group that have specific political or business affiliations. All news houses in India save one, are owned or affiliated to one or the other national or regional political parties.

Hence, the media is primarily serving the interest of investors (the political party or private investor) and the business houses. Even if he TV anchors, journalists and newspaper editors are personally committed to professional ethics of neutrality, they are constrained with the directives and interests of the media owners and commercial advertises or the business houses that provide them revenue. Sold media cannot be a bold media and cannot be useful for democracy and freedom.

The media houses which are 100 % controlled by the political parties influence the people's mind though fear and emotions to propagate their agenda and garner votes and support for the party. Similarly, marketers creating advertising are doing their level best to create hypnotic ads that lure us in, bait us, tickle us, tease us, and then make us take an action that they desire (such as buying their product).

With multimedia such as video, the additional sensory impact makes the hypnotic effect even more prevalent. Our mind cannot handle more information, so our conscious mind faces an overload. This makes our sub-conscious mind ready to accept all suggestions of the media without challenge by our conscious mind.

With the prevalence of internet, and what with the widespread use of smart phones, the influence of mass media on the psyche of people and societies has increased to a great extent. We do not need research to show that Mass media is like the two sides of a coin, exhibiting both positive as well as negative effect. Good or bad effect is directly proportional to the extent of usage.

Media Content- to Inspire Audience

Peer Computer Science journal published a report that states that positive content spread via social media is shared more often and has a far-reaching effect on its audience than the spreading of negative content. Content with a positive spin is more effective with readers or viewers. Using positively motivated communication brings a host of emotions. Some of those may be joy, hope, delight, happiness, excitement, pleasure, and amusement. Those feelings are wonderfully positive, and we can certainly use them to our advantage as well as to benefit our business.

The positive content reminds us of Ramayana, the mythological TV serial with a positive and divine social message based on the Hindu epic, returned to national broadcast portal Doordarshan, amid lockdown with record-breaking viewership numbers. It registered a viewership jump of nearly 40,000%. It became the world's most-watched show on April 16, 2020 with 77 million viewers. The classic show that took the country by storm in the 80s is aimed at encouraging people to stay at home during the country-wide lockdown amid the COVID – 19 pandemic.

A good chunk of content in mass media is negative with violent stories, dire political predictions, and reports on controversial figures or terrorism. In fact, on many occasions, negative content may elicit much more of a response than we anticipate. Even though no one likes to watch something that is unsavoury, research indicates that negative content still has a high viral potential, probably curiosity plays a big role in this.

A question may arise, why does the media telecast or publish news with negative content? Specially TV news & TV serials/soap operas where they have limited viewing time and are forced to air a lot of breaking news and updates on negative stories. Bad news and bad stories stand out – it is peculiar. Nobody would read a story with the headline "50,000 commuters successfully make it to work on time." On the other hand, "Rape Murder, Accident on highway, blocking traffic" is a sensational story that will be reported. Media companies in order to generate revenue through advertisement need to attract more viewership and accordingly they use both positive & negative content.

We can very well conclude how media has made an impact on our mind, right from the print media days right up to electronic media, especially now, in the days of social media like WhatsApp, Facebook, Twitter, Instagram etc.

How to Bring Positivity in Media

So long as media is influencing our mind in a positive way, it is perfectly fine. One way to bring positivity in the media could be awakening of moral sentiment among investors in the media. Other option can be encouraging philanthropic organisations to invest in media houses and harness the energy of movie, music, cartoons, and comic books to spread the positivity with right messages. Challenge lies in how to we energise the artists, activists, and all concerned citizens to bond their commitment and spread positive social messages. Especially, to mention, news channel must show news and not their politically motivated views to create hatred and confusion in the society. It is not out of place to conclude by saying that the birth of private media was necessitated by the need to create awareness among people by showing the gaps in the working of the corporates, private bodies, state and the government. Government run media's work was to talk about the achievement of the state and government. When private news channels begin to act like slaves of political parties, government and private bodies, it makes itself into an entertainment channel of vested interest groups to become most useless for common people and the society.

Part VI

Practicing Creativity

"Imagination leads to
Creativity. Creativity
blossoms into thinking.
When creativity blossoms,
thinking emanates.
Thinking provides
knowledge. Knowledge
results in innovation.
Innovation makes the
nation great."

Dr A P J. Abdul Kalam,

30

Innovations for Future

Discovery Vs Innovation

Innovation is the need of the hour, now, for our survival and development. It is a must for ensuring that everyone can lead a happy and meaningful life. Unless we constantly think about new ways to approach problems and innovate, we will not progress. Innovation is one of the most overrated words in business world today. As of 2014, there were over twenty million 'innovation' search results on Google and more than sixty-five thousand plus books on "innovation" in Amazon.com. It describes everything from incremental improvements in technology to revolutionary or disruptive changes that impact society in a positive way.

Let us understand the difference between invention and innovation. To understand innovation, there are various definitions. According to "Innovation Network, U.S.A." it is defined as "Implementing new ideas that create value". According to "U.S. National Innovation Initiative", it is defined as "The intersection of invention and insight, leading to the creation of social and economic value." Innumerable definitions can be found in literature. What we have chosen to use, is here, adapted from many different sources: "Innovation is the profitable implementation of idea". To sum up… Innovation = Invention + Commercial Exploitation. An invention differs from an innovation at any given time, since it does not have commercial value, but it may do so, in the future. 3 "I" s of innovation are Idea (old/ new), Implementation and Impact. In other words, when an idea which could be either new or old, is implemented, it has impact in the society. For example- An old idea of Non-Violence (very idea coming from Buddhism/ Jainism) was implemented by Mahatma Gandhi in a new way (non –violence movement) for freedom movement with an impact (freedom from British). This is also innovation.

Let us begin to look with one example of how discovery differs from innovation. Albert Einstein was the first to find about LASER (Light Amplification by Stimulated Emission of Radiation) while doing research on radiation. Therefore Laser, a concentrated beam of visual rays was a discovery as it was already there in existence. However, Dr Manilal Bhoumik invented a type of laser called Excimer laser which was used or implemented in eye surgery. The immensely popular Lasik corrective eye surgery came into practice, doing away the need for wearing eyeglasses or contact lenses in many a case. This was implemented with a positive impact in the society. We can say that Laser discovery was not an innovation but the application of "Excimer Laser" for eye surgery (Lasik corrective eye surgery) was an Innovation.

Dr. Geoff Nicholson, the "Father of Post-it Notes" rightly said "Creativity is thinking but innovation is doing, if you have an idea you should have the passion to do something about it". Higher the learning quotient, higher will be the innovation quotient. The more we are equipped with the latest skills, knowledge, learning, studies, and research, the more will be innovations. If learning stops, then innovations stop and ultimately the development stops.

As per the Global Assessment report, approximately one million of Earth's estimated eight million plant, insect and animal species are at risk of extinction, many before the end of the decade. We are facing a human extinction crisis. Fossil fuels and industrial farming have been identified as major drivers of the crisis. Still, we are in the denial mode. To address the issue of pressure on our earth, environment and social challenges humanity is facing, we require a society with a quest for innovations to live in harmony with nature and protect the planet.

To sustain, we need to re-design our future accordingly. There is an immediate need to reduce the energy consumption, reduce production of goods, reduce consumption of goods, double the shelf life of the products, reduce extracting natural resources, stop violence against nature, reduce the environment impact of manufacturing, reduce energy wastage and change our behaviour. We need new ways of doing business, new business model, new process, new system, new ways of thinking, new ways of working, new way of living and evolve a new order of economy: "Minimum Consumption Maximum Well Being". In other words, what we need today is innovation in every sphere of our life. If we do not innovate, we would be forever stuck doing the same old things the same old way. When we say this, we remember the popular theory of creative destruction postulated by one of our favourite economists, Joseph Schumpeter. "The theory of creative destruction" refers to the process by which economic change takes place through the creation of new ways of doing things by virtue of developing from within, hence, destroy and replace the old ways. He argued that innovation, entrepreneurial activities, and market power drives economic change. He also cited, "the rate of progress of any nation depends upon its rate of innovation which in turn also depends on the rate of increase in the entrepreneurial talent in the population". To bring more innovations in any country, we need a greater number of talented and creative entrepreneurs. He argued that technological innovation is directly proportional to temporary monopolies, allowing imbalance in profits that would soon be whisked away by competing rivals and imitators. These temporary monopolies are important to give the motivating force to firms to grow new items and processes.

Need for Innovation in Energy Sector

As per the report of The World Economic Forum, the three biggest hazards to humanity are climate change, extreme weather, and other related environmental factors. The root causes all this problem is the pursuit of cheap energy source. Energy has become so fundamental to improve the quality of our life that we are constantly threatening our planet to extract non-renewable energy and threatening the ecosystem with pollution. In fact, the root cause of war and geopolitical conflict are also related to the control over energy supply. The cheapest source of energy is fossil fuel which has been named among the chief culprits responsible for an environmental crisis. This will continue till the cost of extraction of renewable energy dips dramatically and thereby giving an opportunity to even the poor countries, the access to locally generated renewable energy. This will benefit all countries, including rich and poor, from the perspective of supply certainty and the price front too. The renewable energy system based on solar, wind and waterpower will ensure sufficient and secured supply of energy independent of geopolitical conflict or import price risk. To ensure this, there is an urgent need for innovation to reduce the cost of the renewable energy and to make it affordable to even the poorer countries. We need series of innovations to use existing resources efficiently, to reduce environmental damage, reduce energy consumption and to produce clean energy.

India's LED Lighting Story

The rapid growth of economy and urbanization will compel us to see a significant rise in lighting services in the coming couple of decades. When we talk about innovation in reduction of energy consumption, it is worth mentioning: a light-emitting diode (LED) light bulb, developed in 1962 by Nick Holon Yak Jr., while he was in the employment of General Electric. These bulbs consume 75% less energy compared to incandescent lighting bulbs, 40 % less compared to fluorescent lights and have lasting power 25 times longer than incandescent lighting bulbs. Old fashioned incandescent light bulbs that were energy in-efficient had to be binned. Even the CFL bulbs were no match to the LED bulb. According to a research, "a complete transition to energy efficient lighting would reduce the global electricity demand for lighting by 30–40% in 2030." Industry development policies have been adopted by many countries to spur on a rapid growth in the LED industry. India's LED Lighting story is worth mentioning. In 2014, the government launched a programme to promote LED bulbs in Indian households and later named it "UJALA" (Unnat Jyoti by Affordable LEDs for All). The programme, without compare, the world's largest, has sold more than 270 million LED bulbs, with no subsidy from the government. Would it not be interesting, to learn how this programme has changed India's lighting industry and the subsequent consumer behaviour?

31

Innovations to Address Social & Environment Challenges

Innovation Culture in Organisations

The process of innovation needs a three tired support. The first, at the macro level i.e. national level. Innovation in a nation is directly proportional to the national government's policies and support. The second, is at the level of enterprise or organisation. It is imperative that the top management gives its support and commitment in enterprise. It is the top management of the organisation which sets the policy, direction and enabling environment for the innovation in an organization. The third one is at the base level i.e. Individual level. We could call this the Grass root level. Organizations ought to create multi-functional teams and encourage individuals involved in the innovation process. Activities and inspiration of multifunctional groups and individuals associated with the innovation process would guarantee success in innovation.

One must take a leaf from the page of Minnesota Mining and Manufacturing Company (3M), to understand and truly appreciate the innovation culture at play. 3M is an iconic innovative company in the world. Mostly known for "sticky and scratchy things" (post-its and sandpaper), 3M have over 55,000 innovative products. They released 25 new products per week and over 3700 global patents were granted in 2016. 3M launched its iconic "15 percent program" in 1948, where

15 percent of employees' time was dedicated to innovation. The Post-It note was invented during the "15 percent" time. Similarly, Google has replicated this approach. Google employees are required to spend 20% of their work week on projects that are of interest to them. Gmail and Google Earth made their arrival during Google's "20 percent" time. People are greatly encouraged to work on their ideas. When innovative ideas make it through the ideation phase, employees are given technology grants to pursue their ideas.

What we need today is the innovation culture in the organisations either in government or business to find new solutions with products or services to overcome social and environmental challenge that act as hurdles in the path of finding something new and different.

Interestingly, to foster competition among the countries, there is the "Global Innovation Index "(GII) since 2007. An annual ranking of countries by their capacity and success in innovation, used to compare countries by their level of innovation. It gives innovation performance of various countries in the world. GII 2019, ranks Switzerland as the most innovative country in the world, Sweden, the United States of America (U.S.), the Netherlands and the United Kingdom (U.K.) follow close on heal.

Inclusive Innovations

Let us remind you of the famous quote of Franklin D. Roosevelt, the 32nd president of the United States of America. He said "The test of our progress is not whether we add more to the abundance of those who have too much… it is whether we provide enough for those who have too little" Hence Innovators' heart should strive to bring in change with "out-of-the-box "innovations, work for a larger social cause and benefit the bottom of pyramid population. Desire for innovation should be driven by a search for low-cost solutions to public problems with an objective to ensure that even the poor can afford to have access the innovative product/services. In other words, there is a need for inclusive innovation including meeting the requirement of the bottom of pyramid section of the society. It is worth to a mention a few more successful stories on how enterprise led systemic innovations are offering low cost solutions for the public.

Three-wheeler- Towards Zero Emissions

The e-rickshaw revolution in India has become a game changer and demonstrated it is the potential to become zero emission modes for the masses. It is an affordable vehicle, that is steering the electric mobility revolution in India. This innovative product today has penetrated deep into the rural areas. This is affordable and pollution free. It is interesting to explore how Auto rickshaw was replaced by E-rickshaws. While an e-rickshaw costs only just INR 85,000 (1200 US$), the auto rickshaw cost INR 1.68 lakhs (2400 US$). E-rickshaw runs on batteries. The batteries if charged overnight can operate for 80 kms. The operating costs are significantly lower than the auto-rickshaw. Not to mention the fact that it has reduced pollution significantly. According to available data, the e-rickshaws volume has gone up approximately 1,400 times since 2010. As against 2015, numbers exceeding 16 times more e-rickshaws have been registered in 2017.

With the assumption of improvement in grid emission factors, The Energy Research Institute (TERI) makes a recommendation that a 30 percent change over of the fuel run three-wheelers to electric three-wheelers by 2030 would result in 7 percent reduction in CO2 emissions and a 100 percent conversion by 2050 would result in 18 percent decrease.

Jaipur Foot- Among the Greatest Inventions of the 20th Century

Jaipur foot- a prosthetic foot made from rubber for below the knee amputees was hailed by the Times magazine as being among the greatest inventions of the 20th century. This technology made it easy for the differently abled, to walk bare foot on rough surfaces, run, go cycling, work in the fields, climbing mountains, trees, and do more. It costs just 30 US$, a fraction of $ 10,000 that is charged in western countries. "Bhagwan Mahaveer Viklang Sahayata Samiti" (BMVSS), Jaipur is the world's largest organization, rehabilitating over 1.78 million differently abled people. The articulation at the 'ankle' allows not only inversion-eversion movements but also dorsiflexion (essential for squatting, standing up from prone position, and so on.) Interestingly, Sudha Chandran, an Indian actress and dancer, who lost her limb in an accident, was fitted with the Jaipur Foot, and resumed dancing once again.

Hippo Roller- a Smarter Way to Collect Water

According to WHO & UNICEF, 2.1 billion people lack access to safe readily available water at home implying that it must be collected from elsewhere, most often from a great distance away. Traditional method of collecting water is by balancing on the head, a heavy 20-litre bucket (20kg) mostly by women, children, and the elderly. This daily hardship is very time-consuming as it entails an arduous walk to and from a long distance. Two engineers from South Africa while designing a wheel barrel, realized they could put water in the wheel. This gave rise to the novel idea of the Hippo Roller. What better answer to the people of water-starved communities than by bringing access to water closer to them. This device is used for transporting 90L of water easier and more efficiently than traditional methods. No weight is carried on the head, instead, the water can be drawn by the roll of the drum by manipulating it inward or outward, depending on the gradient.

The "Hippo roller" facilitates bonus 5 times volume of water. The value of this is seen in the way women better utilize this time in and around the house; and it is joyful to see children attending school on a regular basis, resulting in smarter and educated leaders of the future. This has led to improvements to sanitation and hygiene, and prevention of debilitating injuries due to weight bearing, notwithstanding. The sturdy design enables a long lifespan of at least 7 years, if not longer, conditions remaining favourable. This low maintenance structure where there is no wear and tear of parts, proves very effective in sustaining and maintaining long and sustained success in remote rural areas.

Chotukool - Little Cool- Sparking Effect on Bottom of Pyramid

The billion plus people at the base of the Pyramid (BOP) cannot afford to store some milk, daily vegetables, and fruits without letting them spoil and get half a dozen bottles of cold water. Purchase of refrigerators is out of their reach. Is it possible to make this 'essential luxury' affordable and accessible to the people at the Bottom of the Pyramid? To solve this question, Godrej Company's engineers made a field study, to gain deeper understanding of consumer habits and life of the people in the rural India and BOP families. Chotukool was conceived and created, based on many of these vital needs and appreciating invisible insights. Keeping the perishable food items fresh was of paramount importance, not so much the need to produce ice. Keeping this mind, a low-cost portable cooler was developed. The good news is that it uses no compressor or refrigerants. It is portable with a light weight (about 7.8 kg) 43 Litres cooler, that operates on re-chargeable and sometimes, solar power. It keeps daily need food fresh and cool between 5°C to 15° C in the typical ambient temperature in the house. It is priced between INR 3500 (50 US$ approximately) in the market and is affordable to the bottom of the pyramid. It brought smiles on their faces and improved the productivity of the bread winners in BOP homes. This innovation is a symbol of an approach to address the larger issue of Inclusive Growth. This case study on innovation and its impact is being taught in number of business schools, that includes, Harvard University.

Tata Swatch- Ensuring Safe Drinking Water for Masses

The World Health Organization WHO estimates that 80% of diseases worldwide are waterborne. Alarmingly, groundwater in one-third of India's 600 districts is not potable. Dangerous levels of fluoride, iron, salinity, and arsenic are found in the water. With the aim of providing safe drinking water to the masses, Tata Group developed a low-cost, modern, low-maintenance, user-friendly, water purifier for the masses. It uses "rice husk ash" (RHA) impregnated with "nano silver particles" to filter out bacteria and get rid of harmful germs. It uses no running water or electricity to operate. It is the apt innovation for rural poor who have no access to running tap water and electricity. The devise costs INR 1300 (18 US$) approximately. This is an affordable water purifying option for the world's poorest people to eradicate waterborne diseases like diarrhoea, dysentery, cholera, typhoid, and hepatitis etc.

32

Amazing World of Frugal Innovations

Indigenous or Rural People- Often Knowledge Rich But Economically Poor

Unlike systematic enterprise led innovation, a prudent Innovation by an individual or by the community. It is the wisdom of facing harsh constraints, without succumbing, and turning it around into an effective solution albeit with the barest minimum resources available. Bottom of Pyramid people follow this grass root approach to solve daily life problems or meet social needs with simple and quick solutions with limited resources/little expenses. These solutions might not have top notch elegance, sustainability, or scalability. Indigenous or rural people, who are often very knowledgeable, are economically poor. These people know a lot of useful things, but they lack the enterprise to make it work in their favour.

The world needs to emulate India: There was this potter Manubai Sakalani (name changed) who made a prototype of a refrigerator, can you guess with what? Yes, you are right, "Clay!" The magic of this is, it uses no fuel. Fruits and vegetables as well as milk, remains fresh and unspoilt, in this clay refrigerator.

They call Africa the dark continent, but the resourcefulness of the Africans, makes them think out of the box, as well as "think on their feet". Would you ever think of recharging your cell phone, which has gone low on battery, or power has drained fully, using the bicycle dynamo? Peruvian Engineering college students have found a novel way of harvesting water from air, where the climate, in and around Lima city, is extremely dry. Annual rainfall does not exceed one inch. The marvel created by the engineering college was putting up giant billboards, allowing them to soak up the humidity in the air, and in turn converting it into pure water. What gets generated is water in excess of ninety litres daily. More examples of prudent innovations are furnished in the following paragraphs.

Royal Enfield Bullet Motorcycle Into a Modern Plough

When in need, "invent" seems to be a classic case of a Gujarati farmer, in India. Necessity is the mother of invention" rings true in the case of a farmer in Saurashtra region of Gujarat. Cash strapped, the farmer, sat thinking, and when his gaze settled on his motorcycle, he had a moment of enlightenment. This brainwave was what made him modify his motorcycle into a basic yet modern plough. Once, he made it work for him, other farmers, feeling very encouraged, started emulating him.

This is how it all began. Back in 1994, a severe drought in the region forced Jagani's family to sell their bullocks. It was becoming increasingly difficult to find experienced labour to harness the bullocks to till the land, not to mention the inability to absorb the high cost of fodder to nourish those animals. The manpower migration of the farm labourers towards cities aided the adversity concerning agriculture. Jagani's brainwave of converting his Bullet motorcycle to plough the land, gave this farmer cum welder with the expertise to repair diesel engines, hit the jackpot. He reminisces "We had 20 bighas of land, no money and no means to plough it. I got this idea of developing a 'Bullet Santi' ('Santi' means plough in Gujarati) from 'Chhakdas', the common mode of three-wheeler transport in Saurashtra," He removed the rear wheel of his motorcycle and replaced it with a set two smaller wheels that were in turn joined by an "axle". He then attached a plough to the bike and fitted a 5.5 hp diesel engine. The upgraded motorcycle was now "a multipurpose machine that could be used for ploughing, sowing, intercropping, insecticide spraying, also used for transporting small volume of goods.

It was advantageous that when the need arose, it would be easily dismantled into a regular motorcycle. It soon became a smashing "hit" with other farmers. Many farmers in Saurashtra, already owners of motorcycles started emulating Jagani.

Low operation cost boosted Jagani's 'Bullet Santi' into a successful venture: ploughing two acres of land per a litre of diesel in a time span of an hour. This proved to be cheaper than working a tractor. This success saw more innovations brought about by Jagani.

Jagani has a score of converting more than 500 motorcycles till date. Its cost, about Rs.40000 to assemble a Santi, is now patented both in India and the USA.

Issues with Grass Root Innovations

Six key issues face grass root innovators. The first one is the diffusion of these innovations has been extremely slow. The second is lack of networking among the innovators for collaboration. The third is the fact that innovators sometime may not want to become entrepreneurs themselves. The fourth is that innovators lack of access to risk capital. The fifth one which is lack of "intellectual property protection" through proper channels and legal backing designed for helping small innovators. The sixth one is having no access to technical know-how or design input for making their innovations see the light of day, a commercial product.

Despite these issues and adversities, the "unsung heroes" and "heroines" of our society have gone ahead bravely, without any outside help to innovate practices and products for finding solutions to their day to day problems in life. Many of these innovations albeit extremely simple, can improve efficiency of farm workers, of women, small farmers, artisans. Interestingly, In India, these frugal innovations are being scouted, documented, and disseminated by National Innovation Foundation. What we need is the linking of these grass root innovators with the technology and funding agencies to help hem improvise the product/service with due credit to the grass root innovators for their" intellectual property right" (IPR). We may seek support of "one stop facility centres" (OSFs) in rural and urban areas in India and may be in other parts of the world to identify the rural innovators to link them with National Innovation Foundation for making such innovation commercial by improving their outreach.

Innovators- Catalysts for Development

Innovator is focused on his/her idea of introducing something new. So ultimately the nature sticks to its rule of change by causing innovations. Innovators are catalysts of change. We also need the movement of social entrepreneurs to come out with social innovation to address social and environment challenges

We need to develop in all spheres of life with innovative methods. The innovation is more essential for sustainable way of living. Innovation should be for the development of technology for solutions to address the social and environment issues including food security, water, energy and environment, health care and education.

Part VII

Redefining the Knowledge

"We want that
education by which
character is formed,
strength of mind is
increased, the intellect
is expanded and by
which one can stand on
one's own feet"

Swami Vivekananda"

33

Morals and Ethics

Ethics vs Morality

Are morals the same as ethics? Both relate to "right" and "wrong" conduct. While they are sometimes used interchangeably, they are different: ethics means right and wrong as dictated by society/external voices (religious principles/workplace rules/Acts/Law etc.). Ethics are more extrinsic rule sets to guide us all. Ethics are what is right, you obtain for yourself and the good and benefit of all, while morals mean right and wrong as dictated by your conscience/internal voices.

To elaborate on this, take this example: you are taught not to steal. You go into a bookstore and read a magazine while standing up and leave the magazine behind before you leave the store. Morally, you did nothing wrong; you did not steal the magazine. Ethically, this is not right as you read the magazine, acquired the information using your time in the store, without paying for it, thereby deprived the store of one sale. Now, the magazine is technically not new, as you read it, and so now the store is selling a used magazine but charging the next customer a price for a new magazine. Ethically, you stole from the store and the person who ends up purchasing the magazine. So, morally it is not wrong, but ethically it is.

Also moral is an inner voice so we can give an example which would not create conflict with ethics. For Example - I see a beggar on the road daily, ethically I have no obligation to give him something each day, but I give whenever my moral voice becomes stronger than ethical voice, in a similar way when we see someone manhandling a thief we still request them not to hurt the thief but to handover to the law due to our moral values even though, theft is a crime and an unethical act. Similarly, giving tax to government is an ethical and moral value both, as our tax helps the poor and ensures the prosperity of our nation.

All Social Animals Are Capable of Behaving Morally

Scientists have found out that all social mammals are capable of moral behaviour. Studies have found that some social animals like wolf, dolphin & monkeys have ethical codes and are most times willing to help others even if there is no direct gain for them for helping. It has also been observed that some animals offer consolation to individuals in distress. Such behaviour that is due to the empathic nature of the animals. The two main pillars of human morality are reciprocity (the practice of exchanging things or respect with others for mutual benefit) and empathy (sense of compassion). Of course, the human morality is more than this. A few studies have shown that chimpanzees have a sense of fairness.

To cite an example, the world's most famous Primatologist, Dr. Frans de Waal had experimented with chimpanzees to understand the sense of fairness in them. He had two chimps in adjacent cages. One chimp would get to choose from two different tokens. If he chose one colour, he would get a treat, but the adjacent chimp would get none. If he chose the other colour, both would get treats. Very quickly, the chimp controlling the treats would choose the tokens that brought treats to both. Indeed, chimpanzees understand the concept of fairness very well. So, a big question remains unaddressed- If chimps and bonobos lead such moral and ethical lives, why not human.

Ethics Since Ancient Time

Thousands of years ago, stone age hunter-gatherer tribes had moral codes of conduct. Among humans, morality is prevalent in all societies irrespective of religion they follow and practice. In fact, this is prevalent even in the society where no religion is practiced. In other words, religious faith is not a pre-condition to have moral virtues.

Let us examine a few ethical codes which were prevalent in ancient world. Babylonian King Hammurabi introduced Hammurabi code (refers to a set of rules or laws enacted). The laws covered in this Code include "slander, trade, slavery, the duties of workers, theft, liability, and divorce". Hammurabi states that he wants "to make justice visible in the land, to destroy the wicked person and the evil-doer, that the strong might not injure the weak". Torah, the first part of the Jewish bible was well known in the legal and ethical code of Sumerian, Egyptian and Babylonian empire. One of the ten Commandments of the Jewish and the Christian, is "Thou shall not steal".

Dharma (right behaviour) constituted the base of ancient Indian society. Dharma expected a man to live in society as a civilised being, suppressing his selfish urges to the interest of others. It is possible to attain elevated moral values and proper steps to right behaviour when we follow "Dharma". It supports allegiance, faithfulness, and reverence, because "Dharma" is the only path to adhere to. Each of us has an obligation to fulfil. In the Bhagavad-Gita, "Niskama karma" is advocated, because it is something that only focuses on the good of those around us, rather than me. For the Hindus, this law is what they must follow and may also be called" Karma yoga". Other texts namely "Upanishads" and the "Ramayana" propagate morals and morality. When one goes through the "Mahabarata" what comes across are the basics of conscience and the lack of it, as well as truth, peaceful nature, largesse, The concept of right and wrong is at the core of the Mahabharata which emphasizes, among others, the values of truthfulness, absence of anger, charity, sense of pardon, realising of your own self.

In Buddhism, the foundation of ethics are the five rules, which advocate refraining from killing; stealing; lying; sexual misconduct; and intoxicants. Jainism also places great emphasis on three most important things in life, called three jewels "Triratna". These are samyagdarshana ("right faith"), samyagjnana ("right knowledge"), and samyakcharitra ("right conduct").

Sikhism also places great importance to ethics in life. It advocates controlling the Five Evils - "Kam" (lust), "Krodh" (anger), "Lobh" (greed), "Moh" (Material attachment) and "Ahankar" (ego). It also advocates practicing the Five Virtues - "Sat" (truth), "Santokh" (contentment), "Daya" (Compassion), "Nimrata" (Humility) and "Pyaar" (love).

During the battle of Anandpur Sahib in 1704, Bhai Kanahaiya, a follower of Guru Govind Singh, with his love and compassion, poured water into the mouths of the wounded, whether they were Sikhs or soldiers of Mughal army. He blessed them with his hand on their head, and healed the fallen and wounded soldiers, who would then rise and resume battle. This exemplifies the value of non- enmity, service, and compassion.

The Charaka Samhita (Compendium of Indian system of medicine-Ayurveda) emphasises the values of a medical professional. It says, "Those who trade their medical skills for personal livelihood can be considered as collecting a pile of dust, leaving aside the heap of real gold". It also says, "He who regards kindness to humanity as his supreme religion and treats his patients, accordingly, succeeds best in achieving his aims of life and obtains the greatest pleasures".

Chanakya in his book "Nitishastra" (treatise on the ideal way of life) has given practical Lessons of Ethics for Everyone. A wealth of native wisdom, moral and practical advice, is contained in this. Although these were written in the context of the society and the times in which Chanakya lived, many of these codes of conduct are universal in their application. Given below is a selection of verses from "Chanakya Niti"

शरीरस्य गुणानां च दूरमत्यन्तमन्तरम् । शरीरं क्षणविध्वंसि कल्पान्तस्थायिनो गुणाः ॥ Shareerasya gunaanaam cha dooramatyantamantaram Shareeram kshanavidhwamsi kalpaantasthaayino gunaah

What it means is, there is a world of difference between the body and good qualities. The body perishes any minute, but the good qualities live on (Persons are remembered for their good qualities even after death, not for their bodily features).

Ethics in Modern World

Ethics constitute an important part of one's personality. If people stop being ethical in their lives, the whole structure of the society will crumble. Money, power, authority, greed, hunger, and fame among many more, are some of the causes for people's un-ethical behaviour. One interesting social experiment the "Wallet test" shows that Age, sex, or wealth appeared to be no indicator of honesty.

Readers Digest Case Study on Honest Test

"Reader's Digest conducted a test of honesty among hundreds of people in 16 countries, by dropping wallets and recording how many were returned. It discovered that people in Helsinki are the most likely to return a found wallet, and Lisbon residents are the most likely to pocket the cash. Around 200 wallets with a cell phone number, family photographs, coupons, business cards and local currency worth around $50 were dropped in parks, shopping malls and on the pavement in 16 cities: New York, Amsterdam, Berlin, Bucharest, Budapest, Helsinki, Lisbon, Ljubljana, London, Madrid, Moscow, Mumbai, Prague, Rio De Janeiro, Warsaw and Zurich. In Helsinki, 11 of the 12 wallets dropped around the city were returned, the best result. Mumbai residents were the "second-most-honest" people, returning nine of the 12 "lost" wallets. New York City and Budapest came next in the honesty stakes, with eight of the 12 wallets returned. Less honest were residents in Amsterdam and

Moscow, who handed in seven of 12 lost wallets. Berlin and Ljubljana residents handed in six wallets and in London and Warsaw just five wallets were handed in. Residents in Lisbon were the least honest, with only one person handing in the wallet. Ninety of the wallets, almost 50%, were returned. Age, sex or wealth seemed to be no predictor of honesty."

Ethics & Moral values are required at all levels, including in personal life, community, society, government, and business. There is Interdependence between Society & Business. Some of society's problems have been created by corporations such as environmental degeneration, pollution, corruption. An improved social environment with business ethics will be beneficial to both business and society.

Business Ethics

In the late 1980s, European tanneries and pharmaceutical organizations as they continued looking for modest waste-dumping destinations, moved toward Africa's nations on the west coast from Morocco to the Congo. Nigeria, whether out of ignorance or some gain, consented to take on the exceptionally harmful polychlorinated biphenyls (PCB). Unprotected and clueless neighbourhood labourers emptied barrels of PCBs and set them close to a local location. Neither the occupants nor the labourers realized that the barrels contained harmful material.

How can the government permit such abuses by the business houses? In many countries, ineffective enforcement of law combined with inadequate regulations leads to such behaviour by unscrupulous companies.

To cite an example, the privileged developed countries no longer use asbestos. Its toxicity has prompted 52 countries to ban its use. The European Union (EU) has banned it. Asbestos is used in a limited way in products such as automobile brakes and gaskets.

Interestingly, for the past 20 years, two million tons of asbestos a year is being put in homes and schools causing a public health hazard, for decades to come. In India, it is thriving, being the world's second largest asbestos market after China. Efforts to ban asbestos nationally have fallen on deaf ears. "The White Asbestos (Ban on Use and Import) Bill, 2009", introduced in the Rajya Sabha 10 years ago, is still pending in the Upper House.

In January 2009; the Kerala State Human Rights Commission banned the utilization of asbestos sheet material for school structures. Be that as it may, somewhere else, asbestos is viewed as a fundamental for development. In Andhra Pradesh, a pro-asbestos agenda is being pushed by lawmakers who apparently have command more than 25 percent of India's asbestos creation through seven plants across India.

Wrong doings practised in the US banks around 2008 and 2009, had a ripple effect around the world. It led to a worldwide downturn, because the bankers compromised morals by luring bank customers into taking loans which caused real estate boom. What it led to was losses in business, and loss of livelihood.

We see a lot of such scams and misconduct, happening around the world without any care for social impact or reflection. Businesses cannot be successful if the society around them fails. United Nations Development Programme advocated for research framework to examine the ethical and spiritual application by the business enterprises of a Buddhist-based philosophy of "Sufficiency Economy,"

The findings point out, to accomplish long term corporate sustainability; an effective business undertaking should rehearse great moral and profound qualities by means of morals/ethical quality, sensibility, reasonableness, empathy and care for its partners. The pivotal spiritual values embraced in a business context ought to be "integrity, honesty, accountability, quality, cooperation, service, intuition, trustworthiness, respect, justice, and service".

Does Ethics and Business Go Hand in Hand, or They Are Diagonally Opposite?

Research suggests incorporating ethics and spiritual values into the workplace can enhance productivity and profitability as well as employee retention, customer loyalty, and brand reputation. An investigation by the "Performance Group", a consortium of seven leading European companies including Volvo, Monsanto, and Unilever, concluded that producing environment friendly products can enhance profitability, and help win contracts in developing markets.

A study reported in MIT's Sloan Management Review concluded that, "People are hungry for ways in which to practice their spirituality in the workplace without offending their co-workers or causing acrimony".

Those business entrepreneurs who adhere to ethics may grow at a slow pace initially but in the long run, they succeed. Several highly successful industrialists like Bill gates, Henry Ford, Narayan Murthy, Ratan Tata across the world proves that ethics are the only way to be successful in business. Let us quote a famous quotation by Henry Ford "A Business That Makes Nothing but Money Is a Poor Business." It is worth mentioning Swami Vivekananda's message "Western dynamism and efficiency, combined with Indian spirituality can install noble echoes in management of enterprises"

Code of Conduct for Business

Every business should strive to adopt trustworthiness (being transparent and honest in all actions and communications.) Respect for employees and customers, fairness (Treating customers and employees with a sense of fairness and justice), showing a sense of caring. Some of the examples of Ethical Behaviour in the Workplace could be "Putting Customer Needs First, Being Transparent, Prioritizing Workplace Diversity, Respecting Customer Information, providing mechanism of reporting Unethical Behaviour in the company." This will boost internal and external perceptions of the business. In one simple sentence, Warren Buffet Explains the Power of image of a company. One of Buffet's most famous belief statements is, "It takes 20 years to build a reputation and five minutes to ruin it. If you think about that, you'll do things differently."

We need to instil faith in morality and faith in ethics at all levels in the business. No businessman wants his employees to cheat him/her. He would surely expect to see certain ethics in his workers, colleagues, and subordinates. But for it to percolate through all levels, he/she must practise those ethics himself/herself.

Many companies have adopted and instilled the ethical code of conduct. For example, "Tata Code of Conduct" (TCoC), serves as the ethical guideline for Tata employees, and those employees to understand their duties and commitments towards shared values and principle. For generations of Indians and even outside the country, the word Tata had been synonymous with "trust" and "integrity". The group was well known for its corporate social responsibility and principles such as the "Tatas don't bribe" and the "Tatas don't indulge in politics". To uphold value system, the company has been disadvantaged repeatedly, in other words, have lost projects, and sometimes projects have been delayed. Strict adherence to these principles had led to the group prospering under the predecessors of Ratan Tata and him at the helm, saw the company, the best-known Indian group in the world.

Ethics in Government

We often hear the term government ethics. Government ethics are those set of professional code of conduct for the government officials. Government ethics, therefore, involve rules and guidelines defining right and wrong behaviours for a host of different groups, including elected leaders (the Prime Minister, Chief Ministers and Cabinet Ministers), elected representatives and public servants at local, state & central level.

As a part of good governance, a few countries have adopted e-governance OR Smart governance to the efficiency and accountability of the public sector, and tackling corruption. E- governance can be defined as the application of Information Technology to processes of government functioning to bring about a "Simple, Moral, Accountable, Responsive and Transparent governance". However, the elected representatives and the government officials are required to follow the oath taken in the true spirit. This is only possible by instilling the values to them.

Further there is need for developing and enforcing an informal code of conduct for people in high places of responsibility. A line from a Tamil classic reminds us a code of conduct for such people. It says that "if people who are in high and responsible positions, go against righteousness, the righteousness itself will get transformed into a destroyer. Whoever deviates from righteousness, whether they are individuals or states, they are responsible for their own actions".

Elangovadikal (a Jain monk) in his book "Silapathikaram (written nearly 2000 years ago in Tamil language) says the following

"If there is righteousness in the heart, there will be beauty in the character.

If there is beauty in the character, there will be harmony in the home.

If there is harmony in the home, there will be order in the nations.

When there is order in the nations, there will peace in the world."

In the absence of ethics, governance would be clogged with corruption, business with greed and society with violence. We need to work towards eliminating this outcome. To achieve that, we need to spiritualise politics/governance.

Classic Story on Ethics in Governance

"Once, a Chinese traveler came to meet Kautilya (Chanakya). It was dusk and darkness had just started to set in. When the traveler entered Chanakya's room, he saw that Chanakya was busy writing some important papers under the lighting of an oil lamp. There were no bulbs or tube lights in those days since there was no electricity. Chanakya smilingly welcomed his guest and asked him to sit. He then quickly completed the work that he was doing"

But do you know what he did on completing his writing work? He extinguished the oil lamp under which he was writing and lit another lamp. The Chinese traveller was surprised to see this. He thought that maybe this was a custom followed by Indians when a guest arrives at their home.

He asked Chanakya, "Is this a custom in India when a guest arrives at your house? I mean, extinguishing one lamp and lighting the other?" Chanakya replied, "No my dear friend. There is no such custom. When you entered, I was working. It was an official work, pertaining to my empire, my nation. The oil filled in that lamp has been bought from the money from the National treasury. Now, I am talking to you. This is a personal and friendly conversation, not related to my nation; so, I cannot use that lamp now, as it will lead to wastage of the money of the national treasury. Hence, I extinguished that lamp and lit this other lamp, since the oil in this lamp has been bought from my personal money."

34

Re-Energizing Education System

When a Child's Education Does Begin?

Once a young mother approached Aristotle, the most respected teacher in Athens, in Greece. She asked the great teacher "when should I begin training my child so that the child may grow up to be an ideal human being". Aristotle asked, "how old is your child". The mother said, "he is just five years old". Aristotle said "Waste no more time. You are already late by five years". He wanted to mean that it is never too early to start inculcating values in the child. Parents are the first and foremost teachers but also the children's role model and mentor. The mother is the greatest influence on the life of the child especially during the early stages when the kid is in the moulding state. This is because children's minds in their formative years are like clay. It is under her influence that child's character is formed. In other words, the education starts from home.

Pre-School Education

This reminds us of an ancient Greek teacher's saying, "Give me a child for seven years; afterwards, and let God or devil take the child. They cannot change the child".

Maria Montessori, the founder of Montessori method of education, in her book "The Absorbent Mind" says that "if we compare our ability as adults to that of the child, it would require us sixty years of hard work to achieve what a child has achieved in these first three years." During the period from birth to six years, child's brain works in a very different way than an adult's does. At this age, her mind is like a sponge. It absorbs huge amounts of information and everything around her, effortlessly, continuously, and indiscriminately. Over 85% of cumulative brain development occurs prior to the age of six. In other words, children develop 85% of their core brain capability by the time they are five years of age and build on this core foundation for the rest of their life.

Nowadays, there is an early childhood education programme in different countries. In India, early childhood education (ECE) programmes are for the children mostly in the first eight years of their life (the age range may vary) as seen in "Anganwadis", "Balwadis", nurseries, preschools, kindergartens, preparatory schools, etc. Interestingly, an overview of 56 impact evaluation studies conducted on ECE programme across 23 countries found positive impacts on health, education, cognitive ability, and emotional development. Nobel Laureate James Heckman conducted a study on early childhood programme and found that participants in an early childhood program in Jamaica had 25% higher wages, 20 years later. Heckman says, "the return on investment in early childhood is even higher than the stock market from World War II through 2008."

What we need today is enlightened society. In the early childhood programme, education with value system needs to be designed to ensure that the righteousness inside the heart is imparted in young minds. This would lead to the evolution of enlightened society.

Today's Education System

India has always boasted a rich tradition in learning and education ever since ancient times. However, with rapid spread of modern education, time-honoured values are quickly making a disappearing act from lives. The present society and the younger generation are facing serious shortcomings in terms of "moral, ethical and spiritual values". This is because modern education focuses mainly on the intellectual development of children, paying relatively little attention to nurturing their critical thinking, creativity, emotional intelligence, or spiritual intelligence.

Today's education system sees school students having a maximum focus on "how do I pass examination, get a degree and get a job". Swami Vivekananda said that "Getting by heart the thoughts of others in a foreign language and stuffing your brain with them and taking some university degree, you can pride yourself as educated. Is this education?".

The parental and peer pressure to excel in academics leaves little scope for the overall development of children and has stunted their thinking power. Swami Vivekananda believed "that education is not a mere accumulation of information but a comprehensive training for life." He also said that "Education is not the amount of information that is put into your brain and runs riot there undigested, all your life". But in modern education, exactly this is happening. Like students, today both the parents and teachers think that their purpose of life is fulfilled when their children pass examinations, get a job in the urban areas with air-conditioned modern office and earn a lot of money.

Commoditisation of Education

The other aspect is 'commoditisation of education'. Entire education system has been commercialised where the buyers purchase the 'education' at prices. Most of the educational institutions run them for monetary gain. Is it a good policy? Is it an anti-poor and anti-people policy? The privatization of education encourages education sector to be a profit-making industry. With privatization, students are required to pay huge amounts of money to get an education and a job. The poor students are excluded from education from private institutes because of hefty educational fees. Sometimes the poor students are compelled to mobilise fund for their education by seeking loans from banks by mortgaging assets. Parents do not mind paying hefty amount to get a placement with a private contractual job offer. The main incentive for the education is a job with the focus on return on investment on education. Universal values do not matter to them. It is the job offer in the urban area with a lucrative salary that matters the most.

Is Privatization of Education, a Good Policy?

Is privatization of education, a good policy? Is it an anti-poor and anti-people policy? Can education be a business product? Are we justified in conducting business in the name of imparting knowledge? Aristotle says knowledge is one of the most important virtues that define the character of an individual person. If we are to impart this, it is the moral duty of every welfare state to give accessible education to every section of the society. State should not outsource education to private parties and privatize education. Unfortunately, this is exactly what is happening in India and many more countries. Government's policy leans more towards gradually letting the states to withdraw from higher education, based on the broader economic ideology, that it is best to leave higher education be privatized. The private individuals are selling education as per the requirements of the business sectors and norms of the markets. As a result, we have neglected to support educational values, critical thinking and path breaking research & innovation, in our colleges and universities.

On one hand we claim that education is a fundamental right. Universal Declaration of Human Rights, adopted at the UN General Assembly in 1948, declared that "everyone has the right to education". Article 26 in the Declaration stated that "education shall be free, at least in the elementary and fundamental stages" and "elementary education shall be compulsory".

Educating every individual in the world, might help to make our planet a better place to live in, where justice prevails, equality in chances is given to everyone. When we talk of free education, it ought to be early childhood education leading up to secondary schooling. Focus on the development of the person, and ethical way of life, would ensure a much better world. Education only to a select elite individuals ought to be a practice of the past.

Can Information Technology Replace Teachers?

Do we know how the world will look like in 2050, 2075 or 2100? We have no answer. Do we know what kind of knowledge and skill is required in 2050, 2075 or 2100 for livelihoods? How will governments function? We have no answer. Today it is more difficult to predict, because of the high rate of change, in the technology domain. A baby born today will be 30 years in 2050. Therefore, the child's learning today may be outdated and not relevant in 2050. In other words, the knowledge and skill required for their livelihood may not be relevant, but the eternal moral values and ethics will be relevant forever.

Today, where is the knowledge that is lost in information? Where is the wisdom we have lost in knowledge? We are living now in a world of over-communicated environment where in we are bombarded with information (both good & many unwanted messages) daily. In the process the relevant ones are lost in the noise. How can the students absorb it and analyse it?

Students have 24x7 access to smart phones and the internet. They are spending significant amount of time in getting information which is a mix of authentic and untrustworthy. They cannot judge which is correct information is and which is fake. In the process they form their own impression of the world. Teachers cannot be replaced. Teachers will continue to play a very important role in facilitating students to get right information and knowledge and critical thinking. It is the need of the hour for the schools to teach critical thinking and creativity with a special focus on life skills, morals and ethics.

Should We Change the Present System of Education in Our Country?

So, should we make a change in our present system of education in our country"? Or should we improve? It is the need of the hour for the students to inculcate universal values like Integrity, Courage, Respect, Responsibility, Gratitude, Compassion, Caring, Sharing, Generosity, and Service.

Swami Vivekananda once said "We want that education, by which character is formed, strength of mind is increased, the intellect is expanded and by which one can stand on one's own feet. What we want are western science coupled with Vedanta, as guiding motto,…" These words by Vivekananda are still relevant today and represent the true aims of Indian Educational system. Interestingly the UNESCO report "Learning to be" published in 1972 resounds Vivekananda 's idea of education. It reads "The physical, the intellectual, emotional and ethical integration of the individual into a complete man is a board definition of the fundamental aim of education".

It may not be fair to say that efforts have not been made to promote value education in schools. Many schools have Moral Science' or 'Life Skills', packaged as a separate subject, but, in many cases, neither the teachers nor the students take the subject very seriously. It is often perceived as a subsidiary and as simply an unavoidable burden.

We need to bring in the concepts of value in built into the modern education system. Albert Einstein eloquently said, "If you want your children to be smart, tell them stories. If you want them to be smarter, tell them more stories. If you want your children to be brilliant, tell them even more stories". We need to use the art of storytelling to convey abstract value concepts in a meaningful way.

In Japan, the guiding values for children in elementary schools are sympathetic-empathic (omoiyari), gentle (yasashii), socially conscious (shakaisei) and cooperative-harmonious (kyochosei). Elementary social studies themes include community, family, work ethic, community cooperation, and national cultural and social heritage.

The Only True Teacher

Let us look at the teaching community. They are the guardian of the moral values. They play a crucial role in shaping our society. Since we are talking about the need to integrate value-based education in the modern education system; the teachers also need to possess certain qualities to match the requirement. Accordingly, ideally a teacher is expected to be the embodiment of all goodness, emotionally mature, compassionate, fair and appreciative, patient, friendly and agreeable, listening, assertive, good speaker loves the job, respectful, has an air of spirituality about him/her and an exemplary behaviour.

Do We Respect Teachers?

In the ancient days, teaching profession was a noble profession and the most respected one. In the modern world, the teaching profession probably is not celebrated enough. As per the "Global Teacher Status Index" 2018, China and Malaysia are the countries where teaching is held in the highest public esteem. China tops the survey, with an average of 81% are believed to show respect to their teachers as against the world mean percentage of 36, out of 35 thousand people that were asked questions. However, there is a slight improvement to the teachers' status across the world. Out of all the countries wherein the family supports children to take up teaching as a career/calling, China, India, and Ghana are at the top of the chart.

Gurukulam System of Education in Ancient India

It may not be out of place to mention here the famous educational systems practised in India in the ancient times was the Gurukul System which dates to around 5000 BC. Here, emphasis in laid on a young student's intellectual, cognitive, spiritual, and physical wellness. The system looks at a holistic development of a child, inculcating and promoting values of discipline, self- reliance, right attitude, empathy, creativity, brotherhood, humanity, love, and strong ethics. The focus of Gurukuls was on imparting learning to the students in natural surroundings.

The essential teachings in Gurukulam were in subjects like language, science, mathematics, held through group discussions and self-learning. Yoga, meditation, mantra chanting etc generated positivity and peace of mind and encouraged fitness. One had to do chores on their own in order to impart practical skills in them. All these helped personality developments boosted their confidence, sense of discipline, intellect and mindfulness which is necessary even today, to face the world. The Indian education system in the past through Gurukualm produced scholars like "Charaka, Susruta, Aryabhata, Bhaskaracharya, Chanakya, Patanjali and Panini," and many others. Significant contributions came from them, to world knowledge body in diverse fields such as mathematics, astronomy, metallurgy, medical science and surgery, civil engineering and architecture, shipbuilding and navigation, yoga, fine arts and more

Nature & Education

Human beings evolved to grow in natural environments and flourish in it. Nowadays children are suffering from "Nature Deficit Disorder". It is time to cure "nature deficit disorder" (more stress and anxiety, higher rates of obesity and attention deficit hyperactivity disorder (ADHD) in our kids by giving "nature time". Various studies have shown that nature is not just good for health; it improves their learning ability, too.

It is worth to mention that scientists find evidence that being in nature has a profound impact on our brains to increase our attention capacity and creativity. Even small doses of nature can have great benefits. It promotes social connection and creativity. A study done to see the effects of the location on students' learning, the group that took the lessons outdoor or in a garden better assimilated the learning as against the group that was given the lessons in the enclosed class room. How nature enhances creativity is demonstrated by one of the studies conducted by Gregory Batman, of Stanford University. "He and his colleagues proved that hikers on a four-day backpacking trip could solve significantly more puzzles requiring creativity when compared to a control group of people waiting to take the same hike." In fact, it was 47 percent more.

Who Killed Gurukulam System of Education?

Unfortunately, this concept of education was destroyed, and the modern system of education was brought to India in the year 1835 by Lord Macauley. In Macaulay's letter dated 12th Oct,1836, he wrote to his father: "Our English schools are flourishing wonderfully; we find it difficult to provide instruction to all. The effect of this education on Hindus is prodigious. No Hindu who has received an English education ever remains sincerely attached to his religion. It is my firm belief that if our plans of education are followed up, there will not be a single idolater among the respected classes 30 years hence. And this will be effected without our efforts to proselytize; I heartily rejoice in the prospect". Its only purpose was to de-Indianize the Indians and re-orient them to serve the white masters. In other words, the British India government was more interested in producing white collared employees for its administrative machinery to rule rather than enlightening people. It reminds us the proclamation Issued by Lord Harding in 1844. This stated that "in every possible case, a preference would be given, in the selection of candidates for public employment, to those who had been educated in the institutions established for English education".

Do We Need a Gurukul System Back in India?

Many people consider the gurukul system to be informal and unstructured. However, it makes sense to have a holistic system of education by blending modern concept of education with good features of Gurukul system of education. We need a perfect blend of academics and extracurricular activities in mindfulness and spiritual awareness to make the students better individuals.

Conducting outdoor lessons on a weekly basis help students to improve their mood and motivation and lessen the element of fear in them, and they are better equipped to deal with stress, much better than those students who had indoor classroom lessons. Let your children learn from nature and let the classes be conducted in natural settings. Nature has a way of influencing our emotions, instilling calm, peace and serenity and promote creativity.

Interestingly, there is a recent trend of setting up Gurukulam School in India. Lately a few gurukul schools have come up in India. For example, MIT Vishwashanti Gurukul in the city of Pune has attracted many students from all over the world. Similarly, Swaminarayan Gurukul is a leading school transforming the lives of students since 1948. It has campuses in different cities like Hyderabad, Bengaluru, Mumbai, Delhi, and Ahmedabad. To cite another example, Acharyakulam is a school based on Vedic-cum-modern education near Patanjali Yogpeeth, Haridwar in India. It is a residential educational institution for students from grades 5 to 12. It provides modern science apart from Indian culture, Sanskrit and Yoga. They have decided to establish 600 such schools in 600 districts across the country. We need many more such Gurukulam school in India.

Business Ethics in Business School's Curriculum

When we talk of business ethics, what responsibility do business schools have in all this? Business schools have a duty to instil such values in their students. Major business schools emphasize on the need for their graduates to deal with and solve problems with a moral standpoint. Nowadays Business management schools have introduced a subject called "Ethics in management". Ethics education has become a core concept" in business school education and developed into a compartmentalized field of study on its own.

35

Intention and Desire

Need vs Want

Needs are the things which are essential for a person's survival. We need food, we need water, we need clothes and we need shelter. These things are classified as needs because without them it is impossible for us to live. Many people in this world suffer because they are not even able to have these needs fulfilled.

It is very important to differentiate between Need and Want and this really helps us living a happy life. Want is something that a person desires but may not need for survival, either now or later. Needs and wants may differ among people. For example, one person may want to own a car, while another may want to travel to an exotic country. Each person has his or her own agenda of wants, each with a varying degree of importance. Further, wants can change over a period. This is different from needs, which remain constant throughout the lifetime of the person.

There is no limit to human want. Materialistic people fall into this category. These people get so engrossed in their pursuit of materials that they forget the whole essence of life. It is not our fault. The entire global economic system is consumption driven economy. This is based upon an assumption that, economic growth at any cost is must for the prosperity of the society and elimination of poverty. Focusing on economic growth, there is thrust on increasing production of goods, more job creation, increasing per-capita-income and motivating people to buy goods. If in one month, the sale of car is not gone through, we fear that our economic growth may suffer. The entire world is caught in this net. The marketers and the advertisers hypnotise us and add fuel to impulsive purchase fire. Just imagine if the public mood changes and they stop buying too much stuff. The growth of developing countries may collapse. If people realise that buying more and more goods is not improving their lives, they might reduce their consumption, shift from consumption driven happiness and look for other sources of happiness. Then a new order of economic system is likely to evolve in the society. The new order of economy could be "consume less and live more". Question may arise -What could be other sources of happiness? It is worth to mention about a report of "New Economic Foundation of Government of UK". The report prepared with the review of interdisciplinary works of about 400 scientists across the globe to identify the ways of well-being. This report identifies five key actions for one's wellbeing. These are social relationships, physical activity, awareness, learning, and giving. Nowhere does the "materialistic way of life" get reflected in the list.

We need a world where every person should at least have their needs fulfilled. Does that mean that you should restrict buying things that you need only? No, all work and no play can be detrimental to a person, similarly, without enjoyment of life, life can get monotonous. Occasional treats are welcome, provided they are acquired with what you have earned and not with the resources you do not possess. And do not get disheartened or angry when any of your wants is not fulfilled.

Desires- Vedic Approach

The spiritual conflict of having desires in your life, should not mean you are spiritually weak. The Vedas teach that there are four types of desires: artha, kama, dharma and moksha.

First desire is Artha which refers to the desire for wealth through acquisition by proper means and its right use. When we talk about wealth, there are different types of wealth.

Knowledge is the greatest wealth; both material and spiritual. Material Knowledge means the needs, pursuits, and ease, spiritual knowledge to God, soul and our character. Our learning, deeds of the intellect and earthly experience is necessary for material knowledge whereas goodness, kindness, and harmony with everyone is needed for the spiritual knowledge. Another wealth can be called our Health. Physical, mental, intellectual as well as emotional wellbeing constitutes our health. Good nourishment, exercise of the body and mind, and the cultivation of good thoughts are essential to nurture good health. Contentment is wealth too. To be satisfied with what one possesses and not covet more, gives rise to contentment. Practicing honesty, being truthful and harbouring harmony with everyone around us helps us attain contentment. Material Wealth is what is obviously considered wealth, worldwide. Dharma should be kept in context, in the pursuit of wealth. A portion of our wealth should go towards charity and good deeds. Used wisely, one can live a happy life without become consumed by material wealth

The second desire, Kama which refers to pleasure: sensory gratification, comfort, and sensual intimacy. On a wider scale, it means the fulfilment of other material desires also.

The third one is Dharma which is nothing but our purpose of life—the answer we arrive at by asking, "What am I here to do?" Dharma is a comprehensive term which covers an entire range of values. The ten basic principles of Dharma are 1. Forbearance: to remain calm and always composed, 2. Control of mind: full control over the restless and changing mind, 3. Kshama (Forgiveness): is a virtue of those who are physically and morally strong. However, one ought not be too eager to forgive a habitual wrong doer, 4. Non Stealing One should not steal from others or take anything that belongs to others, without paying its proper price and without their permission, 5. Shauch (Cleanliness):-

One should maintain the body, mind and physical environment clean and pure, 6. Wisdom: to gain wisdom through study, self-experience and wise company, 7. Control of Senses: One should keep one's sense (of action and knowledge) under control and become their master. There are five senses of Knowledge and five sense of action, 8. Knowledge: One should acquire knowledge both of physical and spiritual domain from all possible sources, 9. Truth: The practice truth in thought, words and deed, 10. Non Anger: One should try to remain calm and balanced even when provoked.

Finally, the fourth one is Moksha which means attainment of spiritual liberation, or freedom. This is the final objective of human life. It is the state of liberation from misery and pain, one experiences in human life. It is the state of Ananda (perfect bliss) after attaining which nothing more remains to be attained.

Is There An End to Desire?

According to the Vedas, desire is never satisfied by the enjoyment of objects. It grows more and more and rises to the surface, as does fire when fuel is added.

Professor Tim Kasser in his book, "The High Price of Materialism", observes very clearly how our culture of consumerism affects happiness and wellbeing. If we value wealth and material possessions too much, we are at risk of anxiety, depression, difficult relationships, and low self-esteem. Consumerism is, a huge threat to environmental sustainability.

Yoga Teachings says that not all desires are created equal. Everyone has desires, that is not the problem; It is the inability to differentiate the desires that are soul originated, and further your growth, from those neutral or the ones which make us get caught in confusion, conflict or pain.

How do we know whether the source of a particular desire is soul or the ego? It is only possible through spiritual practices like meditation and spiritual education. Our mind is scattered and gets engrossed in the temptations including material objects around us. The more we become aware, the more we get detached from the temptations. When our capacity for meditation increases, our affinity for materialistic way of life also decreases. Even if we bring your intentions and desires to our consciousness, we need to surrender the outcome to nature. We need to cultivate an attitude, that teaches us the understanding, that when things are not going our way, a grander design, or that something better is destined for us.

Harness the Power: Law of Intention and Desire

As discussed earlier, we are in a grand collaboration with the universe. Therefore, by fine tuning the energy content of our own body, we can influence the energy of our extended body i.e., our environment. We can activate this energy influence by two strengths of our consciousness-Attention and Intention.

Accomplished yogis and Rishis are the masters of attention and intention. They can control body's physiology parameters. They can raise their blood pressure, speed up or slow down their heartbeat, increase or decrease the body temperature and bring their respiratory system and metabolic activity to a standstill. British Reporter, Paul Brunton visited India in the twentieth century and met thousands of people from street magicians to Himalayan Yogis to understand the Indian Yoga tradition. The book "A search in secret India" written by him has provided documentation though photographs and videos of the last century spiritual gems like Ramona Maharishi, Paramhans Yogananda, Maa Anandmayi and so on. Paul met a young Yogi called Brama, who demonstrated to him how he can stop breathing completely. It is worth mentioning here another Book "Autobiography of a Yogi" By Paramhansa Yogananda. He has given detailed account of the power of such intention and attention of several yogis he came across.

We can also learn to use the power of law of intention and desire in our life through yoga practices and meditation. We must be clear about our intention and desires we would like to see manifested in your life and review regularly prior to the time of yoga practices and meditations.

Materialist vs Spiritual Objectives-
Can We Reach Both?

Material goals are centered on pleasing our mind, senses, and body. Spiritual goals are centered on pleasing the soul. Spirituality is not goal driven. One should not have a goal to be spiritual. One should not also choose between material and spiritual goals. Spirituality is a path, a way of life. Spirituality is within you, while materialistic things are outside your body and mind. They can be yours, but they are not you. Is being yourself a goal? The more you try to separate yourself from materialistic things/attractions; you will automatically become more spiritual (come closer to yourself). Spirituality is a process. One should focus on process instead of goal or outcome.

Accumulating materialistic possessions will never become an issue, if you are clear that they are just accessories in my life. They are mine but they are not me. Just take spirituality along with you.

36

Quest for Knowledge Society

Ancient Wisdom

Almost anybody can be educated, but wisdom comes from using the mind beyond what one has been taught in a formal setting. Shri Krishna makes a distinction between knowledge and wisdom. He says that knowledge that arises from within us because of spiritual practice is called wisdom. On realization of this knowledge, nothing further will remain to be known.

We believe that ancient wisdom holds the key for the modern life. It is very vital for the advancement of the society. There is a reason why these wisdoms have been passed over from generation to generation, or in other words, they have endured the passage of time. Wisdom is contemporary. It is not edged out by time or location. The wisdom of Veda, Upanishads, Bhagavat Gita, Jewish scriptures and the Bible are till contemporary, today. The words of Marcus Aurelius, Socrates, and many other men and women of wisdom are still alive today. The wisdoms can be applied even now in our today's world and get positive results. They have inspired great inventors and have brought the world to a better understanding.

Let us start with a famous quote by Max Muller, who says: "Whatever sphere of the human mind you may select for your special study, whether it be language, or religion, or mythology, or philosophy, whether it be laws or customs, primitive art or primitive science, everywhere, you have to go to India, whether you like it or not, because some of the most valuable and most instructive materials in the history of man are treasured up in India, and in India only."

Indian literature of ancient times like Veda, Upanishads entails all the minute details of day-to-day existence through spiritual understanding. It is acting like a polestar guiding our contemporary population. Traditionally, in India, we always considered knowledge (vidya) as the only real wealth (dhana). The world has now come to recognize knowledge as the key resource for change. Knowledge has overtaken other factors of production like land, labour and capital as people talk today of a knowledge economy, or more appropriately, a knowledge society.

It is worth quoting from the Veda in the context of knowledge.

MAHO ARNAHA SARASWATI PRA CHETAYATI
KETUNA| DHIYO VISHWA VI RAAJATI
||...... Rigveda (Mandal 1 Hymn 3 Verse 12).

It means that only 'knowledge' can help us learn of the universe, which is as vast as an ocean. It enlightens all minds. Knowledge destroys the darkness of ignorance. Two ways obtaining knowledge are from an able guru and through self-study.

With the attainment of knowledge, the mind becomes enlightened. We must acquire knowledge from all sources and by all means: studying the scriptures, contemplation, meditation, and so on. Scriptures have an invaluable source of knowledge because it is only through their study that our mind is filled with good thoughts. Good thoughts help us towards a virtuous life. This is a sure way for growth of the mind and to acquire eternal happiness and peace.

Nature is the Source of All True Knowledge

Regarding Leonardo da Vinci, 15th century genius, who is known as a great artist, but hardly anyone knows him as a scientist. Among the famous works created by Leonardo are "The Last Supper" and "Mona Lisa". He was not only a great scientist and mathematician, but a magnificent seer as well. Da Vinci was fascinated with everything that was alive; he focused on quantity as well as quality of life. Spirituality ran through the context of his works, being a moral man, he saw godlike qualities in human beings, animals and plants. He practiced vegetarianism. This spiritual force guided his hand and his mind, exalted Leonardo da Vinci as one of the most acclaimed figures in the world of art and intellect. He said "Nature is the source of all true knowledge. She has her own logic, her own laws, she has no effect without cause nor invention without necessity".

Modern Education Combined with Ancient Knowledge and Wisdom

Many concepts in early Vedic philosophy have been backed up with empirical evidence, today. Modern science is just beginning to acknowledge the wisdom of ancient teachings, deep rooted in ancient Vedic texts and Upanishads, all pervasive in the culture of the Indian subcontinent

There is a need to use the wisdom of Chanakya and Bhagavad-Gita in the management of daily life. Similarly, in the western world, Stoic philosophy of Marcus Aurelius is still relevant in the modern world. Marcus was one of the last "good emperors" of Rome who genuinely cared for the well-being of Romans. Marcus Aurelius wrote a manual (for himself) which we now know as the "Meditations." Even though he wrote these words, 2000 years ago, his insights still carry strong weight today.

Two centuries ago, education was the domain of the elitist religious institutions, who in turn preached morality to those who followed them. Everyone needs moral principles for their peace of mind, so they should be part of our education. Modern education combined with ancient knowledge and wisdom is the need of the hour.

37

Connecting with the Spiritual Master and Mentor

Is Hard Work Alone Enough for Success?

Is Hard Work alone enough for success? It is a proven fact that mentors can guide us and help us to achieve success much faster in life, be it in a corporate career, personal development, or spirituality. It reminds us of a famous quote by 17th century spiritual master Guru Gobind Singh - *जिसका कोई गुरु नहीं उसका जीवन शुरू नहीं* (The one who has no mentor, his life has not begun)

If we browse through world history, we will find that most of the prominent personalities had mentors who took care to oversee their progress in their respective fields. Alexander the Great had Aristotle, Chandragupta Maurya of India had Chanakya, Martin Luther King had Dr Benjamin Elijah Mays and Henry Ford had Thomas Edison.

In the days of yore, mentoring meant having a "Guru" and the guru having a "Shishya" or disciple, that was prevalent in Hinduism and Buddhism, also Judaism and Catholicism. A similar equation was important in Sufism too. This helped the disciple (pupil) to become learned. The guru was called "Pir" and was revered.

In India, the concept of mentoring and its practice is not new. It has its roots in Indian mythology. Lord Krishna had `mentored Arjuna in

Mahabharata. We are aware of the wisdom that lord Krishna passes on to Arjuna during the war.

Interestingly, Guru Purnima in India is a day dedicated to Gurus, (Spiritual Master) and devotees who thank them for enlightening them. The Sanskrit word 'guru' has a meaning behind it. 'Gu' stands for darkness and 'Ru' means removing darkness. Guru Nanak said "Let no man in the world live in delusion. Without a Guru, no one can cross over".

In our life, no matter how hard we work, we need to take the help of a mentor who can guide us in this process, so that we will reach our goals quickly. Your mentor can fast track your progress to success by guiding you by sharing their experiences.

Mentoring- Emerging Field in Modern World

Today in the modern world, mentoring is recognized as a highly effective tool for training and development and it is widely used in educational institutions, governmental institutions, universities, and business corporations. It is becoming increasingly common for workplaces to set up entry-level employees with a mentor (or peer mentor). Similarly, at the school / college level, there is mentor mentee programme.

Since the 1980s, mentoring has been an essential part of management training in business corporations. Companies such as Xerox, General Electric, Kodak, Intel, and Avon all have well-established popular mentoring programmes. In fact, 75 % of Fortune 500 companies today offer mentoring programmes.

Mentoring by knowledge & wisdom experts in each field is thriving at the highest levels of business and learning in the field of music, sports, education etc. Mentors may be educators, Sports coaches, Music Instructors etc. All these mentors should be expert with deep knowledge & skill in the field you wish to learn. They must be role models with virtues & moral values and willing to provide support with energy.

Nicknamed 'Dhing Express', Hima Das, a 19-year-old Indian sprinter from Assam, became the first Indian woman, indeed the first ever Indian athlete, to win a gold medal in any format of a global track event at IAAF World U20 Championships. Despite hailing from a poor family background and from a state with poor sports infrastructure, she became the nation's hero. It is her mentor/coach, Nipon Das who played a significant role in her successes.

In another perspective, Ralph Waldo Emerson, 19th century philosopher and poet says, "Every man I meet is my master in some point, and in that I learn of him." Everyone is better than you at something. Somebody else excels in quantum physics the same way as others are superior to me on the understanding of geopolitics. Only humility will allow us to bow down to this fact and in the gigantic learning field of this earth, we should pick up every bit of chance to learn more and only then will we grow.

One can begin with parents and their friends. One should approach them with humility and a desire to accept criticism. For example- When the Ford Motor Company took off; Henry Ford constantly looked to his friend Edison for advice about business strategy and technological research.

Embracing Spiritual Learning

To be able to have professional excellence through mentoring by experts and to improve ourselves, in any field, by learning from others, we need mentors. Then why do we need a spiritual master? To achieve a holistic growth of life encompassing physical, emotional intellectual and spiritual growth, we also need spiritual mentors who can help us in transforming our life, transforming our mind, finding happiness and success in our life.

Many great personalities across the globe have embraced spiritual learning from many spiritual masters. For example, Alfred Brush

Ford, the great-grandson of the legendary businessman Henry Ford, the current owner of the Ford Motor Company had a spiritual mentor "Srila Prabhupada", the founder of "International society of Krishna Consciousness" (ISKON). His life is still guided by the values and learnings from his mentor. Mr. Alfred Ford has been a disciple of his spiritual master since 1974.

A spiritual master with knowledge and wisdom helps people to understand themselves and the world around them. They teach and enlighten us with every word they speak. They express love and care with every gesture they make. We should not approach spiritual master for material gain. A genuine spiritual master will refrain from attracting your attention to him or her; and will not expect absolute obedience or total admiration of you, instead, the master will facilitate you to appreciate and admire the inner self.

Make a firm resolve to progress in your life transformation journey. Make a conscious effort to surrender to the Guru or the mentor who is assisting you in this process. When you have faith in his/her words and sincerely follow his/her instructions, you will make rapid progress and feel the change within. However, to be more effective in the process, you need to be receptive with open mind (without feeling full of our own previous knowledge, prejudices, and opinions) without blocking new insights and awareness.

In the IV chapter of the Bhagavad-Gita, we have Krishna saying, "Just try to learn the truth by approaching a spiritual master. Inquire from him submissively and render service unto him. The self-realized soul can impart knowledge unto you because he has seen the truth". It also reminds us the verse (sloka) from Bhagavad-Gita where Krishna is teaching Arjuna. Arjuna says "Now I am confused about my duty and have lost all composure because of weakness. In this condition I am asking You to tell me clearly what is best for me. Now I am Your disciple, and a soul surrendered unto You. Please instruct me." (Bhagavad-Gita As It Is 2.7).

The fundamental obligations of the disciple are surrender, service, and inquiry. To submit oneself as the guru's servant, teaches humility and obedience. Due to false pride, a disciple may instinctively dislike the idea of obedience, but it is an important component of spiritual life.

The question may arise - Do we always need to be in the physical presence of our guru? Vedic texts speak of two ways of associating with your guru. "Vapuh" means to associate with the guru through physical presence, and "vani", which means "words" or "instructions," and suggests that the disciple associates with his/her guru by listening, assimilating, and acting upon the Guru's instructions.

References

Part I: The Purpose

1. https://sivanandayogafarm.org/yoga-koshas-spiritual-mental-physical-health/ - Yoga and the koshas for spiritual, mental and physical health.
2. https://fitsri.com/yoga/koshas - Koshas: Transcending 5 Sheath to Know the Self
3. https://www.selfhelphealing.co.uk/be-free-from-possessiveness-ego/ - Be free from possessiveness and shrink your ego
4. https://sivanandayogafarm.org/yoga-koshas-spiritual-mental-physical-health/ - Yoga and the koshas for spiritual, mental and physical health.
5. https://www.osho.com/read/osho/osho-on-topics/ego - How to sacrifice the ego?
6. https://vedanta.org/2003/monthly-readings/the-ego-and-the-self/ - The ego and the self.
7. https://sicohen.wordpress.com/2013/07/16/are-we-really-that-selfish-self-interest-vs-egoism/ - Are we really that selfish? Self-interest vs. Egoism
8. https://weareallsacredbeings.com/blog/what-really-is-the-ego - What really is the ego?
9. https://phuket-meditation.com/attachment-detachment-differences/ - Attachment and detachment- The differences

Part II: Power of Infinity

1. Joseph Murphy, Power of your Subconscious mind- (Mumbai, Embassy Books, 2010)

2. https://soi-seattle.org/the-five-aspects-of-prayer-and-the-five-elements/ The five aspects of prayer and the five elements

3. https://www.yogajournal.com/teach/purifying-the-five-elements-of-our-being Purifying the five elements of our being

4. http://dallasyogafest.org/2017/07/11/the-5-elements-of-nature-and-their-relationship-with-the-human-body/ The 5 elements of nature and their relationship

5. https://chopra.com/articles/the-gayatri-mantra-for-enlightenment The gayatri mantra for enlightenment

6. https://timesofindia.indiatimes.com/astrology/mantras-chants/meaning-and-significance-of-the-gayatri-mantra/articleshow/75065013.cms Meaning and significance of the gayatri mantra

7. https://soi-seattle.org/the-five-aspects-of-prayer-and-the-five-elements/ The five aspects of prayer and the five elements

8. https://liveanddare.com/sufi-meditation Sufi Meditation

9. http://www.happeemindz.com/the-power-of-your-belief-system The power of your belief system

10. http://www.cathryngoodman.com/prayer_is_power Prayer is power

11. https://www.truthstar.com/worship-agni-fire-to-spark-up-your-daily-life/ Worship Agni (Fire) to Spark-up your daily Life

12. http://www.sathyasai.org/devotional/gayatri Gayatri Mantra

13. https://liveanddare.com/sufi-meditation- Sufi Meditation

14. https://ich.unesco.org/en/RL/baul-songs-00107 Baul songs-Intangible heritage

15. https://www.mdpi.com/2077-1444/10/5/335/html Songs of the Bauls: Voices from the Margins as Transformative Infrastructures

16. https://www.huffpost.com/entry/music-spirituality_b_3203309 Music and spirituality
17. https://en.wikipedia.org/wiki/Inayat_Khan - Inayat Khan
18. https://www.sipri.org/media/press-release/2019/world-military-expenditure-grows-18-trillion-2018 World military expenditure grows to $1.8 trillion in 2018

Part III: The Cosmic Realization

1. Paramhansa Yogananda, Autobiography of a Yogi-(New York: The Philosophical Library, 1946)
2. https://yogainternational.com/article/view/understanding-prana Understanding Prana
3. https://www.yogajournal.com/teach/purifying-the-five-elements-of-our-being- Purifying the Five Elements of Our Being
4. https://sheelaa.com/aura-kirlian-photography-scanning/
5. https://www.teslasociety.com/tesla_and_swami.html Tesla and Swami
6. https://theecologist.org/2018/nov/20/embracing-spirituality-scientific-mind Search Results Embracing spirituality with a scientific mind
7. https://bharathgyanblog.wordpress.com/2020/01/07/nikola-tesla/ Nikola Tesla
8. https://swarajyamag.com/books/the-connection-between-vivekananda-tesla-and-the-akashic-field The connection between Vivekananda, Tesla and Akashic field
9. https://www.scienceandnonduality.com/article/the-influence-vedic-philosophy-had-on-nikola-teslas-idea-of-free-energy The Influence Vedic Philosophy Had on Nikola Tesla's Idea of Free Energy
10. https://www.huffpost.com/entry/eating-high-vibrational-f_b_7596472 Eating High-Vibrational Foods for Good Health and Longevity

Part IV: Sustainability for Co-Existence

1. Vandana Shiva; Kartikey Shiva, Oneness vs the 1 %- (New Delhi: Women Unlimited, 2018)

2. https://en.wikipedia.org/wiki/Aral_Sea –Aral Sea

3. https://foodprint.org/issues/pesticides/ Pesticides in our food system

4. https://www.intechopen.com/books/beekeeping-and-bee-conservation-advances-in-research/impacts-of-pesticides-on-honey-bees Impacts of Pesticides on honeybees

5. https://www.forbes.com/sites/paulrodgers/2014/09/09/einstein-and-the-bees-should-you-worry/#6bda3aaa8157 Einstein and the bees. Should you worry?

6. https://livinghistoryfarm.org/farminginthe40s/pests_01.html Search the Dawning of the Chemical Age for Pesticides during the 40s

7. https://allianceforscience.cornell.edu/blog/2017/11/organic-farming-can-feed-the-world-until-you-read-the-small-print/ Organic farming can feed the world — until you read the small print

8. https://www.greenbiz.com/article/indias-farmer-network-saving-seeds-climate-change India's farmer network is saving seeds from climate change

9. https://www.cbsnews.com/news/greta-thunberg-climate-change-speech-at-davos-watch-live-stream-today-2020–01–21/ Greta Thunberg- Climate change

10. https://www.orfonline.org/expert-speak/india-rebuilds-economy-time-make-circular-sustainable/ - As India rebuilds its economy, it is time to make it circular and sustainable

11. https://www.vox.com/future-perfect/2019/6/8/18656710/new-zealand-wellbeing-budget-bhutan-happiness - Forget GDP — New Zealand is prioritizing gross national well-being

12. https://www.intechopen.com/books/nitrogen-fixation/nitrogen-fertilization-i-impact-on-crop-soil-and-environment- Nitrogen fertilization impact on crop, soil and environment
13. https://www.techvshuman.com/2016/08/15/gross-domestic-product-vs-gross-national-happiness-gdp-vs-gnh/ Gross domestic product vs Gross national happiness

Part V: Invisible Challenges

1. Word Development Report 2019
2. Global wealth report 2019
3. Yuval Noah Harari, 21^S lessons for the 21st Century - (London:Penguin Random House, 2018)
4. https://www.wired.co.uk/article/china-social-credit-system-explained The complicated truth about China's social credit system
5. https://business.blogthinkbig.com/can-big-data-help-reduce-deforestation-in-the-amazon/ Can big data help reduce deforestation in the amazon?
6. https://www.fastcompany.com/90272858/how-our-data-got-hacked-scandalized-and-abused-in-2018 – How our data got hacked, scandalized and abused in 2018
7. https://www.theatlantic.com/technology/archive/2011/06/united-nations-declares-internet-access-a-basic-human-right/239911/ United Nations declares internet access a basic human right
8. https://economictimes.indiatimes.com/markets/commodities/news/farmers-fear-loss-not-arrest-and-seed-illegal-bt-cotton/articleshow/69867576.cms?from=mdr Farmers fear loss, not arrest, and seed illegal Bt cotton- June 20th,2019
9. https://www.investopedia.com/articles/active-trading/081315/3-reasons-why-chinese-invest-africa.asp The 3 Reasons Why Chinese Invest in Africa

10. https://www.thehindubusinessline.com/opinion/points-of-law-in-the-pepsico-potato-case/article27060326.ece# Points of law in the Pepsico potato case May 7th, 2019

11. https://theleaflet.in/a-nation-for-farmers-niti-aayog-maharashta-part-iii-nishant-sirohi-pepsico-monsanto/ A Nation for Farmers

12. https://indianexpress.com/article/business/farmers-union-protest-government-decision-to-waive-off-trait-fee-on-bg-cotton/ Farmers union protest government decision to waive off trait fee on BG Cotton, March 31st, 2020

13. https://www.thehindu.com/opinion/op-ed/a-perfect-storm-in-the-cotton-field/article23357894.ece A perfect storm in the cotton field

14. https://medium.com/@vikrammalla/the-politics-of-indian-media-houses-by-ownership-82ecbe2dafab The Politics of Indian Media Houses

15. https://www.spectator.com.au/2018/09/are-multinationals-now-more-powerful-than-the-nation-state/ Are multinationals more powerful than the nation?

16. https://corporate.walmart.com/newsroom/2019/04/23/walmart-releases-2019-annual-report-and-proxy-statement-   Walmart Annual Report

Part VI: Creative Thinking

1. https://india.mongabay.com/2019/08/a-social-venture-on-the-road-to-improve-lives-reduce-emissions-with-electric-rickshaws/ A social venture on the road to improve lives and reduce emissions with electric rickshaws.

2. https://www.downtoearth.org.in/blog/pollution/three-wheel-powered-solution-to-dirty-air-63465 Three-wheel powered solution to dirty air

3. https://www.empowering-people-network.siemens-stiftung.org/en/solutions/projects/hippo-water-roller/ Hippo water roller: Empowering people

4. https://ideas.ted.com/the-genius-of-frugal-innovation/   The genius of frugal innovation

5. https://cprindia.org/news/6527- India's LED Lighting Story

6. https://www.theclimategroup.org/news/new-un-report-confirms-urgency-led-lighting-adoption-globally LED New Un Report Confirms Urgency of Led Lighting Adoption Globally 4th July,2017

Part VII: Redefining the Knowledge

1. https://www.forbes.com/sites/bruceweinstein/2018/02/27/is-there-a-difference-between-ethics-and-morality-in-business/#3e77ec982088 Is there a difference between ethics and morality in business.

2. http://ageofmontessori.org/why-your-childs-brain-is-like-a-sponge/ Why your child's brain is like a sponge

3. https://greatergood.berkeley.edu/article/item/six_ways_nature_helps_children_learn Six ways nature helps children learn

4. https://www.researchgate.net/publication/298784181_Vivekananda_and_the_Making_of_Enlightened_Citizen_An_Explication Vivekananda and the making of enlightened citizen: An Explication

5. https://www.studyinternational.com/news/where-in-the-world-are-teachers-most-respected-asia/ Where in the world are teachers most respected?

6. https://timesofindia.indiatimes.com/blogs/desires-of-a-modern-indian/the-importance-of-the-gurukul-system-and-why-indian-education-needs-it The importance of gurukul system and why Indian education needs it. March 8th, 2019

7. https://euromentor.eu/mentoring/history/ Mentoring: History

8. https://back2godhead.com/role-disciple/ Role of the discipline: Harvard Divinity School

www.ingramcontent.com/pod-product-compliance
Lightning Source LLC
Chambersburg PA
CBHW021353210526
45463CB00001B/95